DREAM CARS

pil

Publications International, Ltd.

PHOTOGRAPHY:

The editors would like to thank the following people and organizations for supplying the photography that made this book possible. They are listed below, along with the page number(s) of their photos.

Chan Bush: 30; **Mirco DeCet:** 118-119, 122-123; **Steen Fleron:** 41; **Gary Greene:** 48-49; **Sam Griffith:** 44-45; **Jerry Heasley:** 52-53; **Don Heiny:** 66-67; **Bud Juneau:** 34-35, 56-57; **Milt Kieft:** 10-11; **Bill Kilborn:** 20-21; **Vince Manocchi:** 6-7, 12-13, 14-15, 26-27, 36-37, 40, 62-63, 64-65, 70-71, 102-103, 106-107, 110-111, 117, back cover; **Doug Mitchel:** 18-19, 31, 42-43, 74-75, 80-81, 82-83, 94-95; **Mike Mueller:** 38-39, 60-61, 68-69, 72-73, 76-77, 78-79, 96-97, 100-101, 104-105; **David Newhardt:** 50-51, 84-85, 112-113; **Gary Smith:** 32-33; **Mike Spencer:** 8-9; **David Temple:** 16-17, back cover; **Phil Toy:** 24-25, 54-55, 109; **Nicky Wright:** 28-29, 58-59, 64, 86-87, 88-89, 90-91, 92-93, 98-99.

ADDITIONAL ART:

Shutterstock.com: 108-109, 116-117

OWNERS:

Special thanks to the owners of the cars featured in this book for their cooperation.

John J. Appelhanz: 8-9; **Dennis Babcock:** 48-49; **Larry Bell:** 90-91; **Dan Bennett:** 78-79; **Don and Carol Berg:** 32-33; **Rodney Brumbaugh:** 74-75; **The Brumos Collection:** 18-19; **Jerry and Carol Buczowski:** 86-87; **Rick Cain:** 98-99; **Steven Capone:** 31; **Cars of San Francisco:** 24-25; **Luis Chanes:** 84-85; **Bernie Chase:** 36-37, 110-111; **Classic Cars of La Jolla:** 112-113; **Freda Cooper:** 56-57; **Greg Don:** 102-103; **Richard A. Emry:** 58-59; **Gordon Fenner:** 16-17, back cover; **Alfred Ferrrara:** 10-11; **Al Fraser:** 80-81; **Bob Fruehe:** 6-7; **Frank Gallogly:** 66-67; **Gil Garcia:** 54-55; **Allan Gartzman:** 44-45; **Denis Gatson:** 40; **Torben Hansen:** 41; **Henry Hart:** 38-39; Dr. **Ernie Hendry:** 20-21; **Jeff Knoll:** 94-95; **Fredrick Knoop:** 76-77; **Mark Levin:** 100-101; **Dr. L. Philip Lufty:** 28-29; **Bob Macy:** 52-53; **Guy Maybee:** 42-43; **Steve Maysonet:** 72-73; **Paul McGuire:** 60-61; **Bruce Meyer:** 62-63; **Motor Cars, Ltd:** 31; **Andrew Peterson:** 82-83; **Robert J. Pond Automobile Collection:** 65; **John Poochigian:** 14-15; **Hilary Raab:** 64; **Lloyd and Karen Ray:** 31; **James L. Roman:** 34-35; **Darryl Salisbury:** 88-89; **Roger Schmeling:** 96-97; **Candy and Tom Spiel:** 70-71, back cover; **Jeff Stephan:**106-107; **Dr. Robert Sutter:** 12-13; **Jeffrey A. and Silvia Sykes:** 109; **Chris Teeling:** 68-69; **Dennis Urban:** 46-47; **George Watts:** 26-27; **William Whitney:** 30; **Stephen Witner:** 92-93.

Special thanks to the following manufacturers who supplied us with additional imagery.

Aston Martin Lagonda Limited, Bugatti Automobiles S.A.S., Ferrari S.p.A., Ford Motor Company, General Motors Company, Automobili Lamborghini S.pA., McLaren Automotive, Porsche AG.

CONTENTS

1909-27 FORD MODEL T 6
1932 CHEVROLET CONFEDERATE 8
1936 DUESENBERG SSJ 10
1936 JAGUAR SS-100 12
1941 CHEVROLET SPECIAL DELUXE 14
1949 FORD 16
1952 MASERATI A6GCS 18
1953 CHEVROLET CORVETTE 20
1955 CHEVROLET BEL AIR 22
1955 FORD THUNDERBIRD 24
1956 MERCEDES-BENZ 300SL GULLWING 26
1957 JAGUAR XKSS 28
1958 CHEVROLET 30
1958 FORD THUNDERBIRD 32
1959 BMW 507 34
1962 FERRARI 250 GTO 36
1962 PONTIAC CATALINA SUPER DUTY 421 38
1963 JAGUAR E-TYPE 40
1963 PLYMOUTH 426 WEDGE 42
1963 PONTIAC SUPER DUTY 421 44
1964 OLDSMOBILE CUTLASS 4-4-2 46
1964 PONTIAC TEMPEST GTO 48
1965 FORD MUSTANG 50
1966 CHEVROLET CHEVELLE SS 396 52
1966 DODGE CHARGER 426 HEMI 54
1966 PONTIAC GTO 56
1966 SHELBY GT-350 58
1967 CHEVROLET CAMARO Z28 60
1967 SHELBY COBRA 427 SC 62
1968 FERRARI 365 GTB/4 DAYTONA 64
1968 FORD GT40 66
1968 FORD MUSTANG 428 COBRA JET 68
1968 OLDSMOBILE HURST/OLDS 70
1968 PONTIAC GTO 72
1969 AMC HURST SC/RAMBLER 74

1969 CHEVROLET CHEVELLE COPO 427 76
1969 CHEVROLET NOVA SS 396 78
1969 DODGE CORONET R/T 80
1969 DODGE SUPER BEE SIX PACK 82
1969 FORD MUSTANG MACH 1 428 COBRA JET 84
1969 CHEVROLET YENKO CAMARO 427 86
1970 AMC AMX 88
1970 DODGE CHALLENGER T/A 90
1970 DODGE CHARGER R/T HEMI 92
1970 FORD MUSTANG BOSS 302 94
1970 PLYMOUTH AAR 'CUDA 96
1970 PLYMOUTH ROAD RUNNER SUPERBIRD 98
1970 PONTIAC FIREBIRD TRANS AM 100
1971 CHEVROLET CHEVELLE SS 454 102
1971 DODGE CHARGER R/T HEMI 104
1972 LAMBORGHINI MIURA SV 106
1973 PORSCHE 911 CARRERA RS 108
1975 LAMBORGHINI LP400 COUNTACH 110
1990 CHEVROLET CORVETTE ZR1 112
1990 LAMBORGHINI DIABLO 114
1992 DODGE VIPER 116
1992 JAGUAR XJ220 118
1994 ASTON MARTIN DB7 120
1996 MCLAREN F1 122
2001 CHEVROLET CORVETTE Z06 124
2002 LAMBORGHINI MURCIELAGO 126
2003-04 FERRARI ENZO 128
2004 PORSCHE CARRERA GT 130
2005 BUGATTI VEYRON 132
2015 CHEVROLET CORVETTE Z06 134
2016 LAMBORGHINI AVENTADOR S 136
2017 BUGATTI CHIRON 138
2017 FERRARI LAFERRARI 140
2017 FORD GT 142
2018 MCLAREN 720S 144

1909-27

FORD

MODEL T

It was on October 1, 1908, just about a month before William Howard Taft was elected President of the United States, that the Ford Motor Company, then barely five years old, unveiled the machine that many historians think of as the most significant automobile of all time. Henry Ford called it the Model T. Introduced as a 1909 model, it was only built as an open touring car at first, but within a few months, other body styles were added to the line. Strictly a utilitarian vehicle, the Ford took no beauty prizes, and it won no speed contests. Still, its 22-horsepower 4-cylinder engine could propel the Model T to a top speed between 40 and 45 miles per hour, adequate for the era's mostly unpaved roads. Widely known as the "Tin Lizzie," the Ford became the butt of a thousand jokes. But it was this machine, more than all the others combined, that was responsible for putting America—and the world—on wheels. On the strength of the Model T, Ford's yearly production increased from 10,000 in 1908 to nearly two million 15 years later. As early as 1913, Ford outproduced all other American automakers combined. The formula for the Model T's success was basic: It was simple, it was tough, and it was cheap, but not cheaply built. The first Model T sold for $825, but the price was steadily reduced as output increased. By 1924, a brand-new Ford could be purchased for as little as $260. When the final T was built in 1927, more than 15 million had been produced.

1932
CHEVROLET
CONFEDERATE

Sturdy, stylish, and brimming with value, the 1932 Chevrolets helped General Motors hold fast through the worst of the Great Depression. As the economic storm battered the company's higher-priced lines that year, Chevrolet would be the only GM division still making a profit. As was Chevy's custom at the time, the '32 models underwent another name change for the year, this time to Confederate. A more efficient downdraft carburetor boosted the sturdy "Stovebolt" six to 60 horsepower, a gain of 10, and a new "Silent Second Synchromesh" transmission virtually eliminated gear-grinding shifts. Despite the improvements, Chevy car sales dropped nearly 50 percent. One casualty of the dismal sales numbers was the Landau Phaeton, a unique "bustleback" convertible-sedan body style that had debuted just a year before. It attracted a mere 1602 customers for 1932, and thus did not return for 1933.

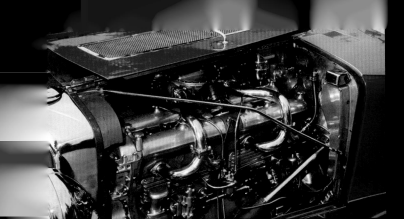

After achieving fame for their winning race-car engines, brothers Fred and August Duesenberg teamed with tycoon E.L. Cord to create "the world's finest motorcar." Bowing in late 1928, the Duesenberg Model J was big, heavy, opulent, and ultra costly, but also America's fastest, most technically advanced car. A supercharged SJ soon followed with at least 320 bhp and up to 140 mph flat out. Shown here is one of two short-chassis SSJ roadsters with the engine tuned to produce 400 bhp. It was as close to a sports car as a Deusey ever got.

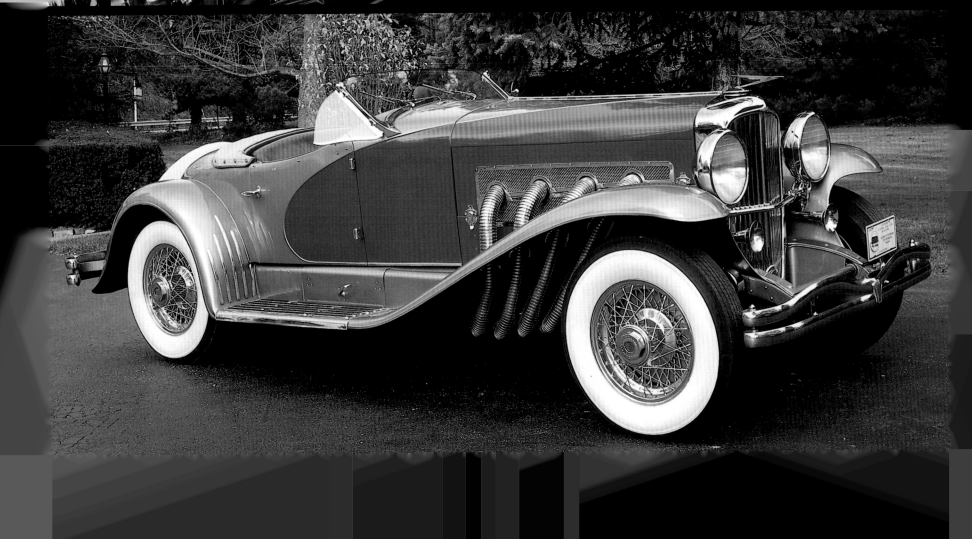

1936
JAGUAR
SS-100

The first sports car named Jaguar appeared in 1936 from William Lyons' SS Cars, Ltd., an outgrowth of Swallow Sidecars, the motorcycle-sidecar business he started in the 1920s. A follow-up to the previous year's SS90, the SS-Jaguar 100 came with either a 2.7-liter straight-six or a new, more potent 3.5-liter unit. The latter could deliver 0-60 mph in under 11 seconds and over 100 mph flat out, sensational for a non-supercharged car in those days. Handling and roadholding were first rate, too. The styling—classically correct but sleek and slow slung—was largely Lyons' own work. Alas, only 314 of these cars could be built before war came to Britain in 1939.

1941
CHEVROLET
SPECIAL DELUXE

America was out of the Depression by 1941, largely due to increased military production prompted by an alarming new war in Europe. Industry heeded President Roosevelt's call to become an "arsenal of democracy," which all but eliminated unemployment but brought on inflation. Chevrolet proudly rolled out its 16-millionth vehicle, a Special DeLuxe Sport Sedan. Though clearly evolved from 1940, the '41 Chevys sported a more sharply raked windshield, in-fender headlamps, and a definite "big car" look over-all. Indeed, many still regard the 1941 Chevy as a sort of scaled-down Buick. Not surprisingly, the $949 convertible coupe remained the style leader; it was Chevrolet's lone drop-top offering, and it came only in top-line Special DeLuxe trim. Production hit 15,296.

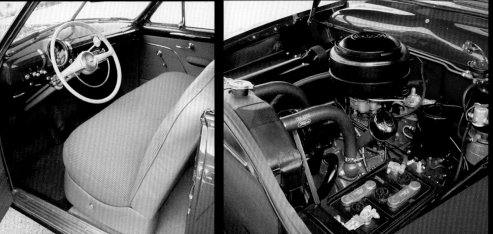

Ford sales for 1946–48 had been healthy—more than 429,000 units for 1947 alone—but the cars were moving because of Ford's enormous dealer network, and the public's postwar hunger for anything new, even facelifts of Ford's bulbous 1942 design.

Organizational deficiencies left by the late Henry Ford were bleeding the company of cash, and independents the likes of Hudson, Studebaker, and Kaiser had taken the immediate-postwar design lead.

The slab-sided '49 Ford was the result of a design competition mounted by company president Henry Ford II, who knew that the postwar seller's market wouldn't last much longer. In-house staff and outside designers were invited to pitch ideas. Indie designer George Walker brought in Richard Caleal (a veteran of GM and the Raymond Loewy design house), Joe Oros, and Elwood Engel. When Caleal became disenchanted with the group's direction, he left to labor independently at his home in Indiana. Set up in his kitchen with clay modelers Joe Thompson and John Lutz, Caleal perfected his design.

Henry Ford II and other company execs viewed proposals created by Caleal, Ford styling chief E. T. "Bob" Gregorie, and Oros and Engel. The Caleal car was chosen, and it went into production virtually unchanged save for a flip of the taillights from vertical to horizontal, with fairings that integrated them into the rear quarters. The new car made its GM and Chrysler rivals look old.

Ford enjoyed its best sales in nearly 20 years: more than 1.1 million units produced during the extra-long model year. Lower and lighter than the '48s, the '49 had a modern ladder-type frame with Ford's first fully independent front suspension. Its 239.4-cid, 100-horse flathead V-8 lent itself to aftermarket hop-up, and noise and handling problems that came with the rush to production were addressed as the design carried though for 1950 and '51.

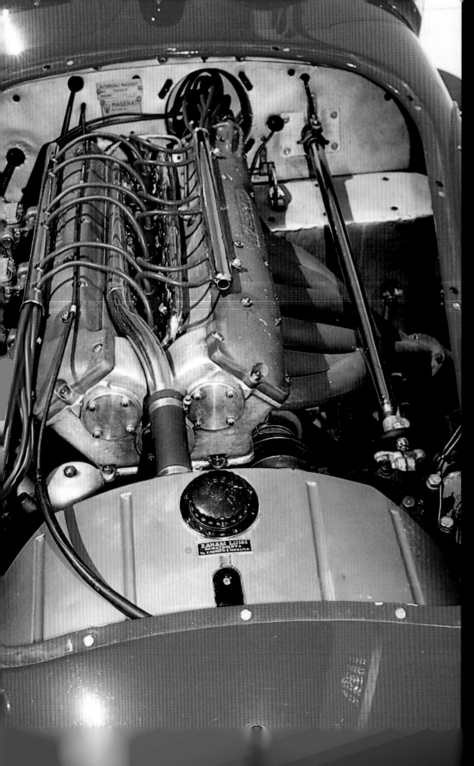

MASERATI
A6GCS

The Maserati A6GCS was an ambitious combination racecar and sports car. The 2.0-liter overhead-cam inline six sat in a tubular-steel frame and initially delivered 120 bhp. But that was no match for Ferrari in European formula racing, so Maserati added a twincam head. With triple Weber carburetors and two spark plugs per cylinder, the engine now developed 160 horsepower. The first cars had cycle fenders, but later cars (such as the one illustrated here) had graceful pontoon-type front fenders that flared out from the grille for better aerodynamics. The fenders could be easily unbolted to create an open-wheel racer for Formula 2 racing. An improved "Series II" A6GCS with modern slab-sided styling appeared in 1953.

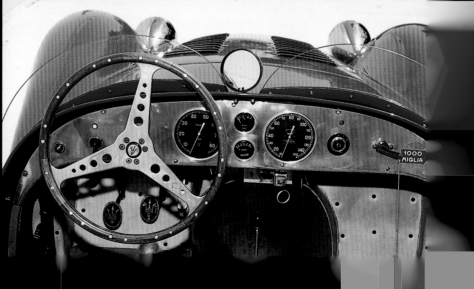

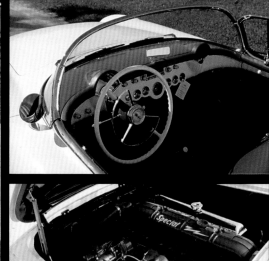

During 1951-52, CM design chief Harley Earl envisioned a two-seat sporty car that could be sold for about $1850, the price of a new Chevy sedan. With practical and morale-boosting support from new Chevy chief engineer Ed Cole, Earl sold top CM management on a fiberglass-bodied roadster that would alter Chevy's rather staid image. The subsequent 1953 Motorama show car called Corvette morphed, without significant alteration, into the production '53 Corvette.

Corvette was sleek and low. Unfortunately, a big reason for Chevy's staid image was its lack of a truly hot engine. Although Cole's team was at work on a V-8, Corvette's first engine (1953-55) had to be based on Chevy's 235.5-cid "Blue Flame" inline six. Producing just 108 or 115 hp in base and uprated form, respectively, the motor was tweaked with triple carbs, solid valve lifters, and a higher-lift camshaft. All of that, plus an improved compression ratio of 8.0:1 (from 7.5:1) brought output to 150 hp (155 for 1954-55).

Although no beast (0-60 mph in 11 seconds), the pumped-up six was nevertheless too much for Chevy's manual transmission, so all '53 'Vettes had a two-speed Powerglide automatic.

A new X-member chassis was strong, but the suspension was basically the same as what Chevy had been using since 1949, albeit with revised shock rates.

As manufacture began, CM became concerned about the fiberglass, which mandated slow, careful assembly that limited production to 50 cars a month. Total Corvette production for '53 was 315. Even at $3250 retail, all 300 were pre-sold.

The first Corvette was widely praised for its low center of gravity and stability in the twisties—hallmarks of European sports cars that didn't emphasize acceleration anyway.

The following year, about 1500 '54 Corvettes remained unsold, and the car was perilously close to being canceled. It wasn't, of course—and became America's longest-running sports car.

1955
CHEVROLET
BEL AIR

Aside from its fresh, dazzling styling, the 1955 Chevrolet's biggest news was its all-new V-8 engine. Designed by veteran GM engineers Harry Barr and Ed Cole, this new "Turbo-Fire" engine pioneered an innovative block-casting technique that made for uncommon manufacturing precision, especially in the low-priced field. With the standard two-barrel carburetor, the efficient Turbo-Fire offered 162 lively horses from 265 cubic inches and a mild 8.0:1 compression ratio. Available dual exhausts and four-barrel carb boosted horsepower to 180, and a racing-oriented 195-hp setup was added late in the model year. Despite its superior horsepower output, the new V-8 ended up weighing 40 pounds less than Chevy's familiar "Blue Flame" six-cylinder powerplant. The Turbo-Fire transformed Chevy's image from dull family car to a dynamic performer that ads appropriately termed "The Hot One."

1955 FORD THUNDERBIRD

The 1955 Thunderbird is one reason Chevy's Corvette avoided cancellation in its earliest years. Simply put, Chevy couldn't allow its roadster to be shown up by Ford's sporty V-8 T-bird.

And Ford knew it could not resist the challenge presented by Corvette's 1953 debut. Although legend holds that the 'Bird was conceived when Ford execs admired British and Anglo American sports cars at the 1951 Paris Auto Show, Ford had had a two-seat concept in the works for some time. Corvette appeared in January 1953. Ford, with preliminary work already complete, was determinedly hard at work just a month later on what would become the Thunderbird.

The T-bird had a traditional steel body, roll-up windows, and a power top or lift-off hardtop. In top trim, the 'Bird's 292-cid V-8 developed 198 hp, a figure that would rise to 202 hp for 1956, the year that brought a 312 V-8 rated at 225 hp.

For 1957, the last year of the first Thunderbird generation, the 292 was rated at 212 horsepower, the 312 at 300/340 (supercharged). Maximum Corvette horsepower for 1955 (its first year with a V-8) was 195, from 265 cubic inches. By '57, the top Corvette powerplant, a 283-cid V-8, produced 283 horses in top trim—57 fewer than Thunderbird.

Though snug on a 102-inch wheelbase (the same measure as Corvette's, by the way), Thunderbird was obviously a Ford, with rakishly hooded headlamps, straight-through rear fenders with discreet fins, a wrapped windshield, and round tail lights.

The efforts of engineer Bill Burnett and young designer Bill Boyer paid off enormously, as first-year 'Bird production was 16,155—enough to outsell the '55 Corvette by a margin of nearly 24 to 1. Production leveled to 15,631 for 1956, and then surged to 21,380 for 1957. Thunderbird had struck like lightning.

1956
MERCEDES-BENZ
300SL GULLWING

One of the most recognized and coveted of sports cars, the Mercedes-Benz 300SL "Gullwing" coupe was evolved from the 1952 SL prototypes that won that year's Le Mans 24 Hours and marathon Mexican Road Race. U.S. import-car baron Max Hoffman convinced Daimler-Benz to offer a production model by ordering 1000 of them. As on the racers, the flip-up doors stemmed from the need to preserve rigidity in a high-sided multi-tube space-frame chassis, but they were distinctive and would be much copied in later years. The only engine was a 3.0-liter six with mechanical fuel injection. Horsepower was a stout 240, fed through a four-speed gearbox. Unveiled in early 1954, the Gullwing sold for a princely $7000-plus. That and its semi-handbuilt nature conspired to limit production to around 1400 units.

1957
JAGUAR
XKSS

Among the raciest sports cars ever, the Jaguar XKSS was essentially a roadgoing version of the Le Mans-winning D-Type, with only the barest concessions to off-track driving. Among them were a larger windshield, windshield wipers, an opening door for the passenger, and a rudimentary folding top. Yet the D-Type was surprisingly tractable and civilized on the street, so the XKSS was too. It was also about as swift, capable of 0-60 mph in under five seconds and a sub-14-second standing quarter-mile. Unfortunately, a mere 16 of these cars were completed when Jaguar decided to end production of both the SS and D-Type following a disastrous factory fire in February 1957. Despite its greater rarity, the XKSS went racing just like its track-bred sister, usually running in production classes, occasionally as a sports/racing prototype. Though no one knew it at the time, the XKSS forecast the general look of the future roadgoing E-Type. Also predictive was the hood/front fenders assembly that tilted up to provide fast, easy powertrain access, a boon in the heat of competition.

1958

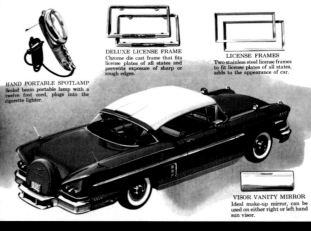

HAND PORTABLE SPOTLAMP
Sealed beam portable lamp with a twelve foot cord, plugs into the cigarette lighter.

DELUXE LICENSE FRAME
Chrome die cast frame that fits license plates of all states and prevents exposure of sharp or rough edges.

LICENSE FRAMES
Two stainless steel license frames to fit license plates of all states, adds to the appearance of car.

VISOR VANITY MIRROR
Ideal make-up mirror, can be used on either right or left hand sun visor.

1958
CHEVROLET

The larger, softer-riding '58 Chevys lost some of the edge their predecessors had in motorsports events, but still could deliver healthy performance when equipped with the new 348-cubic-inch V-8. The regular four-barrel "Turbo Thrust" version made 250 horsepower, while the "Super Turbo-Thrust" delivered 280 horses with triple two-barrel carbs or 315 with high-compression heads and solid lifters. A recession hit the U.S. economy just as 1958 models hit showrooms, and Chevrolet suffered like most other Detroit makes. Model-year production slid to just over 1.1 million, down 363,450 units from '57. Even so, Chevy reclaimed its rank as "USA-1," besting archrival Ford by some 154,500 cars. Volume would go even higher for '59.

1958 FORD THUNDERBIRD

Rather unexpectedly, Ford Division general manager Robert McNamara expressed support in 1955 for the Thunderbird. But he wasn't enamored of the T-bird's two-seat configuration and niche status. What he valued was the growing equity of the Thunderbird name, which he figured could be leveraged into a four-place 'Bird.

That's precisely what happened for 1958, and although sports car purists howled (some are howling still), the 1958-60 Thunderbird was a beautiful, swift, and sportive car with smartly crisp lines that earned it the affectionate nickname "Squarebird." It was also a significant force in the new "personal-luxury" segment that would blossom later with Mustang, Buick's '63 Riviera, and others.

In a reversal of normal practice, Ford Division's design department, headed by Bill Boyer, laid down the basics of the new Thunderbird—not the staff in engineering. Ground clearance of just 5.8 inches mandated a high transmission tunnel that Boyer's people turned into the car's primary longitudinal structural unit. Further, as far as Squarebird occupants were concerned, the hump was a smart-looking console fitted with climate controls, power-window switches, and a radio speaker.

Additional rigidity came from a massive cowl, a reinforced rear deck and rear quarter panels, and chassis rails riding six inches deep to create a recessed cabin floor. Unibody construction and an all-coil Ford-Aire suspension also contributed to this very competent package.

The sole engine was a potent 352-cid V-8 rated at 300 horsepower, mated to a column-mounted three-speed manual, a manual with optional overdrive, or three-speed dual-range Cruise-O-Matic. Famed *Mechanix Illustrated* tester "Uncle" Tom McCahill ran a '58 'Bird from zero to 60 in 9.9 seconds—good for the day, particularly for a car that weighed the better part of two tons.

The hardtop coupe could be had for $3631 in 1958; the convertible coupe for $3929. By 1960, prices ranged from $3755 to $4222, with sales healthier than ever.

1959 BMW
507

Bavarian Motor Works struggled to resume its auto business after World War II, offering an odd mix of high-priced sedans and inexpensive license-built microcars. Yet somehow BMW managed a sleek two-seat convertible in late 1955. Designated 507, it borrowed the basic chassis and running gear of the then-current 502 "Baroque Angel" sedan and related 503 sporty coupe, but a trimmer 97.6-inch wheelbase supported handsome styling by German-American industrial designer Albrecht Goertz. With a 3.2-liter V-8 sending 150 horsepower through a four-speed gearbox, the 507 took just 8.8 seconds 0-60 mph and could do over 120 mph, impressive for the 2900-pound heft. In a sense, this was BMW's Thunderbird, but also an answer to the Mercedes 300SL—and just as costly at about $9000. Only 253 were built, mostly by hand, through 1959.

1962 FERRARI
250 GTO

A true race and ride Ferrari, the 250 GTO was announced in early '62. Though it used the same basic chassis as the SWB 250 GT Berlinetta, the GTO—"O" for homologato, approved for GT-class racing—had less weight, more power from a race-proved 3.0-liter V-12, and superior aerodynamics. New U.S. world driving champ Phil Hill teamed with Olivier Gendebien to win the GT class and place second overall at both Sebring and Le Mans in '62. Only 39 GTOs were built through 1964, including a few 4.0-liter and "Series II" models, plus special-body Prototype-class racers. Surprisingly docile yet very fast—5.9 seconds 0-60 mph, 0-100 in 14.1—the GTO still reigns supreme among collectible Ferraris.

1962 PONTIAC
CATALINA SUPER DUTY 421

tiac was vague on their output, but estimates ranged from 373 to 405 bhp. These were among the largest-displacement mills offered at the time, and they helped spark Detroit's cubic-inch war.

NHRA rules changes for '62 required engines and body parts for the stock classes to be production pieces. This forced the 421 onto the official equipment sheet as an expensive, limited-run option. Fewer than 180 were built for '62, its peak production year. Most went into Catalinas, though 16 or so were installed in Pontiac's new personal-luxury coupe, the Grand Prix.

The '62 Super Duty 421 was officially rated at 405 bhp, but real output was closer to 460. Though street-legal, these again were race-ready engines, with four-bolt mains, forged rods and crank, solid lifters, and NASCAR heads. Stock-car-racing versions used a single four-barrel, but street/strip Super Duty 421s had twin Carter 500-cfm four-barrels and an aluminum intake manifold. Free-flow cast-iron headers were fitted with easily removable exhaust dumps. Only three- and four-speed manuals were offered; Pontiac's automatic wasn't strong enough.

Reinforcing the division's hard-nosed performance attitude were a host of Super Duty options, including aluminum front-end body clips and a weight-cutting modified frame (the famous drilled "Swiss Cheese" frames wouldn't come until '63). These saved about 110 pounds. To shave another 40 pounds, the factory would fit aluminum exhaust manifolds. They were intended only for quarter-mile competition; Pontiac warned that subjected to more heat, the headers would melt.

Super Duty 421 Catalinas were fearsome, and could dip into the 13s at more than 100 mph in the quarter—superior numbers for a regular-production car of the day.

1963 JAGUAR
E-TYPE

A singular sensation on its 1961 Geneva, Switzerland, debut, Jaguar's slinky E-Type—called XKE in the US—picked up the general look and modified unit construction the firm had firs employed for its late-1950s racing D-Type and roadgoing XKSS. Styling was again the work of Malcolm Sayer and overseen by company founder Sir William Lyons. Initially, the E-Type came with the same 3.8-liter six and all-disc brakes of the XK150, while gaining independent rea suspension. A bigger-bore 4.2-liter took over in 1964. This added 23 pound-feet of torque (to 283) but left horsepower unchanged at 265. Starting in late 1967, modifications were phased in to meet federal regulations resulting in the Series II of 1969. Larger bumper and taillights o the Series II, but with triple carburetors of the Series I, identify this yellow convertible as a 1968 Series "1 1/2" US model, as do the "safety" rocker switches on its dashboard.

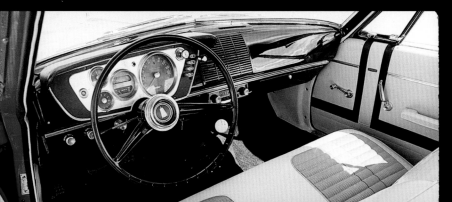

Dodge's one-year flirtation with downsizing ended for 1963, and its big models returned to the 119-inch wheelbase. Plymouth stuck with the 116-inch span, but both divisions cleaned up the styling. No sign of fickleness under the hood, however, where the devastating new 426-cid Wedge awaited.

This was basically a bored 413, again called the Ram Charger at Dodge and the Super Stock at Plymouth. Dual Carter four-barrels and the upswept ram's-head exhaust headers were retained. But the 426 got a host of internal beef-ups to make 415 bhp on 11.0:1 compression or 425 bhp on 13.5:1. Stage III 425-bhp versions followed during the year with further modifications including larger-bore carbs, recast heads, and 12.5:1 compression.

Preferred transmission was a heavy-duty TorqueFlite automatic, which again used pushbutton gear selection. The alternative was a floor-mounted three-speed manual; Chrysler didn't yet have a four-speed. Available axle ratios ranged from 2.93:1 to 4.89:1.

This was serious ordnance, ill-suited for everyday use. Indeed, brochures warned that the 426 was "not a street machine" but was "designed to be run in supervised, sanctioned drag-strip competition....Yet, it is stock in every sense of the word."

Plymouth offered the 426 Wedge in all full-size models, from the sleeper Savoy to the luxury Sport Fury, and even made available a race-ready aluminum front-end package that trimmed 150 pounds.

Mopar's most-popular street performer in '63 was the 330-bhp 383-cid V-8. But the 426 Wedge was there for the asking. *Hot Rod* fueled a 13.5:1-compression version with 102 octane and took it to the Pomona dragstrip. Running a TorqueFlite with a 4.56:1 gear, the magazine smoked a 12.69-second ET at 112 mph.

1963
PONTIAC
SUPER DUTY 421

Pontiac poured on so much performance for '63 that only an order from the highest power could slow it down. Unfortunately, that's what happened.

Super Duty 421s were back, tougher than ever. Compression jumped from 11.0:1 to 12.0:1, while other tweaks increased maximum shift points by 500 rpm, to a screaming 6400 rpm. The four-barrel version, set up for sustained high speeds, had 390 hp. The dual-quad drag variant—now with aluminum exhaust manifolds standard and steel manifolds optional—was again underrated at 405 hp. A second dual-quad drag rendition was introduced with a 13.0:1 squeeze. Pontiac timidly rated it at 410 hp.

Factory weight-cutting again included aluminum front-end pieces and was joined by the famous Swiss Cheese frames, which had grapefruit-size holes drilled into the chassis rails.

Super Duty 421s came only with a Hurst shifted three- or four-speed manual. Axle ratios up to 4.44:1 were offered. Dealers were advised to warn customers to maintain a minimum idle speed of 1000 rpm to insure adequate lubrication; that the engine would be cantankerous in cold weather, noisy all the time, and expensive to run; and that the large oil pan reduced ground clearance.

For those unwilling to take the Super Duty plunge, Pontiac introduced two new 421s that were more streetable. These High Output 421s had 10.75:1 compression and 353 hp with a four-barrel or 370 hp with three two-barrels.

Big Ponchos got new sheetmetal for '63, highlighted by trendsetting stacked headlamps. Pontiac was a force on the street and strip, while in NASCAR, it fought to retain its crown against the brutal new 427-cid Chevrolets.

It was all too much for GM. In January 1963, the corporation withdrew from organized racing and killed the Super Duty engines. Just 88 '63 Super Duty V-8s made it out the door, but Pontiac was poised to open a new performance frontier.

1964 OLDSMOBILE CUTLASS 4-4-2

A case can be made that the very first muscle car was the 1949 Oldsmobile Rocket 88, created when Olds shoehorned its 135-bhp big-car V-8 into a midsize model. When Pontiac rejuvenated the concept with its 1964 Tempest GTO, Olds was compelled to respond. It took until midyear, at which time Olds extended its Police Apprehender Pursuit package to its new intermediate-size F-85/ Cutlass series, which shared the Tempest/ Le Mans chassis.

The package used the top engine available in these Oldsmobiles, a 290-bhp 330-cid V-8, then added a high-lift cam, dual-snorkel air cleaner, and some other minor tweaks to come up with 310 bhp. The engine's four-barrel carb, in combination with the package's Chevy-built Muncie four-speed manual and the car's dual exhausts, gave the new option its name, 4-4-2.

Offered on any body style except the station wagon, the 4-4-2 package added $285 to an F-85 or $136 to the uplevel Cutlass. It included a heavy-duty suspension with anti-roll bars front and rear, plus

"tiger paw" tires. Balanced manners were a goal from the start and some road testers called this new Oldsmobile the best-handling midsize car in the GM stable.

With the standard 2.54:1 axle ratio, a 4-4-2 turned a respectable 15.6-second quarter-mile at 89 mph for *Car Life*. By comparison, a 290-bhp Cutlass was two seconds slower to 60 mph and 1.3 seconds slower in the quarter.

But where Pontiac successfully pitched its GTO to the youth market as a factory hot rod, Olds was more tentative in promoting its new muscle car; one of the few advertisements pictured a couple of cops in a four-door F-85 sedan that didn't even wear the tri-color 4-4-2 badge. Performance buffs just weren't used to looking at Olds, and only 2999 4-4-2s were sold this first season. Pontiac, by contrast, moved more than 32,000 GTOs in '64.

1964 PONTIAC TEMPEST GTO

The Big Bang in modern muscle's evolution is the 1964 Pontiac GTO. This is where it began: a midsize automobile with a big, high-power V-8 marketed as an integrated high-performance package—the very definition of the muscle car.

To create the GTO, Pontiac sidestepped GM's prohibition on intermediate-size cars having engines over 330 cid. In a ploy that didn't require corporate approval, Pontiac made its 389-cid V-8 part of a $296 option package for the new Tempest. The name Gran Turismo Omologato was boldly appropriated from the Ferrari GTO. Roughly translated, it means a production grand touring machine sanctioned for competition.

Pontiac hoped to sell 5000 '64 GTOs; it sold 32,450. The Goat, as it was affectionately dubbed, generated a cult following and sent rivals scrambling to come up with similar machines.

To create an engine worthy of its original, Pontiac fortified the 389 with a high-lift cam and the 421-cid V-8's high-output heads. The GTO had 325 bhp with the standard Carter four-barrel. About 8250 of the cars were ordered with the extra-cost Tri-Power setup—three Rochester two-barrels—and were rated at 348 bhp. Both versions had 10.75:1 compression and 428 lb-ft of torque. The standard three-speed manual and optional four-speed used Hurst linkages; a two-speed automatic also was optional.

A thick front sway bar, heavy-duty shocks, stiffened springs, and high-speed 14-inch tires were included. A $75 "roadability group" added sintered metallic brake linings and a limited-slip diff. The sporting attitude carried over inside, where all GTOs got bucket seats and an engine-turned aluminum instrument surround.

Four-barrel Goats typically ran 0-60 mph in about 7.5 seconds and the quarter in 15.7 at 92 mph. Tri-Power GTOs were consistently quicker and added immeasurably to the car's mystique.

1965
FORD
MUSTANG

Mustang is the car that changed everything, proving the existence of a youth market ready to be turned on by a sporty personal car (Falcon underpinnings notwithstanding) that could be optioned from six-cylinder mild to V-8 wild. It's one of the greatest of all automotive success stories.

The archetypal '65 Mustang is the hardtop coupe, a car that most clearly shows off the aggressive yet pretty long-hood/short-deck proportions by Joe Oros, L. David Ash, and Cale Halderman. The car remains beloved as well as respected, and thousands of examples are proudly driven today. And although clearly a "youth" car, the hardtop's purity of design also lent itself to appeals to chic sophistication.

The '65 Mustang fastback became available on October 1, 1964, fewer than five months after the coupe and convertible (the last, the priciest Mustang, at $2614) appeared in dealerships. Initial fastback badging said "MUSTANG 2+2," and although two people could be squeezed into the back seat beneath the sharply sloped roof, bags of groceries might feel more at home. The side-rear "window" vents were functional air extractors.

Base fastbacks were equipped with a 200-cid, 120-hp inline six, which was sufficient to move the 2589-pound 2+2 around town with OK briskness. Drop in the small-block 289 V-8, though, and you had a different animal altogether. During this first model year, more than 77,000 fastbacks found homes.

The GT (for Gran Turismo) was the performance Mustang and was intended to suggest drivers' adventurous, even aggressive, spirit. Most GT packages had the 225-hp 289 with four-barrel carburetor and a three-speed, fully synchronized stick shift. The GT's front disc brakes were particularly useful if the buyer opted for the 271-horse version of the 289, with 4-speed stick (the latter an oxymoronic "mandatory option"). The stronger 289 had optional "short" rear axle ratios (3.89:1 and 4.11:1), which made the cars enormously appealing to street and strip drag racers.

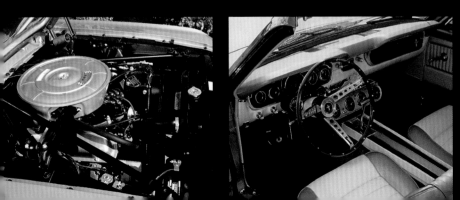

1966

CHEVROLÉT

CHEVELLE SS 396

Chevy repositioned its Super Sport Chevelle as an all-out performance car for '66, but in some ways, more turned out to be less. Like other GM intermediates, it was reskinned, though dimensions hardly changed. SS models got a blackout grille and a new hood with nonfunctional vents. With engines of around 400 cid now obligatory in this game, Chevy made the 396-cid V-8 standard, so all its midsize muscle cars were now Chevelle SS 396s.

But instead of the 375-bhp Z-16 396 that bowed midway through the '65 model year, the '66s got detuned 396s rated at 325 bhp in base Turbo-Jet guise and 360 bhp in optional L34 form. Both new mills had 10.25:1 compression, but the L34 got a taller cam, stronger block, and larger four-barrel. It cost $105 extra and nearly one-third of SS 396 buyers ordered it. Still, the L34's mid-15s at around 90 mph in the quarter were pretty ordinary.

So was much of the rest of the car, at least compared to the pricey limited-edition Z-16. Instead of reinforced brakes and underpinnings, the '66 SS 396 used standard Chevelle brakes and suspension pieces. Chevy claimed it had stiffer springs and shocks—an assertion some testers disputed once they experienced the car's wayward handling and subpar stopping ability. In fairness, comfortable seats, tractable engines, sporty styling, and a $2776 base price made the '66 SS 396 a great daily driver.

Then, in the spring, Chevy released the L78 396. This was essentially an updated Z-16, but with solid lifters and new exhaust manifolds. It had the 427-cid V-8's large-valve heads, plus 11.0:1 compression, aluminum intake manifold, and an 800-cfm Holley. The L78 echoed the Z-16's 375-bhp rating and was the 396 that hard-core Chevy street warriors had hoped all the '66s would be. Only about 3100 L78s were built. But even the base Chevelle SS was now a genuine big-block muscle car, and the best was yet to come.

Plymouth's 1964 Barracuda was America's first modern fastback, beating Ford's '65 Mustang 2+2 to market by about two weeks. Dodge waited until '66 to join the fray, and then leaped in with muscle other fastbacks could only dream of.

Built on the midsize Coronet platform, the new Charger added a rather graceless fastback roofline, hidden headlamps, and full-width taillamps. With a base price of $3122, it cost $417 more than a Coronet 500 hardtop. Part of the deal was a state-of-the-art '60s interior: lots of chrome, four bucket seats (the rears folded down), available center consoles fore and aft, and full gauges.

A 318-cid V-8 was standard. The most-common performance upgrade was the optional 325-bhp 383 four-barrel, which would push a Charger through the quarter in the low 16s at 85 mph. But 1966 was also the year Chrysler's 426-cid Hemi V-8 came to the streets, and it made for the ultimate Charger.

Actual horsepower was near 500, but Dodge advertised its Street Hemi at 425 bhp on a 10.25:1 compression. A detuned version of the 12.5:1-compression race Hemi, the new customer version retained solid lifters, but had a milder cam for smoother low-rpm running and a heat chamber so it could warm up properly. It also mounted its dual quads inline, rather than on a cross-ram manifold. The engine added $1000 to the price of a Coronet, or $880 to a Charger, and included stiffer springs and bigger (11-inch) brakes. Front discs were optional.

"Beauty and the beast," was how Dodge pitched its new Charger with the hot 426. "The Hemi was never in better shape," it boasted. Of 37,344 Chargers built for '66, however, only 468 got the Hemi. Maybe that's because Hemi buyers got a one-year/12,000-mile warranty instead of Dodge's usual five/50,000. Even that, Chrysler warned, would be voided if the car was "subjected to any extreme operation (i.e., drag racing)." Heaven forbid.

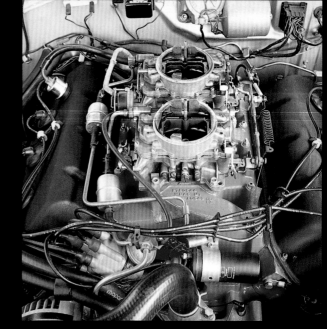

1966 PONTIAC
GTO

Recognizing the CTO's growing popularity, Pontiac promoted it from a Tempest option to a model of its own for '66. The Coat rewarded Pontiac with sales of 96,946 units, the highest one-year total ever attained by a true muscle car.

Credit for its success was twofold. Other CM divisions had copied the CTO with hotter versions of their intermediates, but like Ford's new Fairlane CT, none captured the Coat's all-around appeal. Mopar had the performance, but no special muscle models. And while all CM midsize cars were restyled for '66, none matched the beauty of the CTO's voluptuous new Coke-bottle contours.

Wheelbase was untouched, and overall length and curb weights changed negligibly. But styling highlights included a graceful new roofline and cool fluted taillamps. The unique CTO grille had mesh-pattern inserts made of plastic—an industry first.

The standard hood scoop remained nonfunctional, but Tri-Power engines could again get an over-the-counter fresh-air kit, and a few were equipped with the Coat's first factory Ram Air. A small number of CTOs were ordered with a boss new option: weight-reducing red plastic inner fender liners. Inside, the new instrument-surround was genuine wood.

The four-barrel 389 continued at 335 bhp. The $113 triple-two-barrel had 360 bhp (with or without Ram Air), but production ceased at midyear when CM outlawed multi-carb engines for all but the Corvette. Three- and four-speed manuals and a two-speed automatic could be had with factory axles spanning 3.08:1 to 4.33:1.

Car Life's four-speed four-barrel with 3.08 gears and air conditioning ran a 15.4 quarter at 92 mph and got 12.4 mpg. The magazine said the lightly loaded rear wheels of its nose-heavy test car would "skitter and skip on anything but the driest pavement." Braking power was poor, but the shifter was sweet, the motor willing, and assembly quality high. That, and that beautiful new body, obviously was the formula for success in '66.

1966
SHELBY
GT-350

At Ford's behest, Carroll Shelby turned the hot-selling Mustang "ponycar" into a serious race machine, the CT-350. Modifications abounded, including a stripped-down fastback body, beefed-up chassis, and a tuned 289 V-8 rated at 306 horsepower. A track-ready R-model packed at least 325 bhp. Both were high-performance bargains at $4547 and $5950, respectively. Shelby built 562 CT-350s for '65 and 2378 of the similar '66s, including 936 CT-350H models like this. The "H" stood for Hertz, which lost a bundle on weekend rentals.

1967 CHEVROLET
CAMARO Z28

The Sports Car Club of America's Trans American sedan series was the premier racing showcase for pony cars in the late '60s, and Chevy had to score there to hurt the entrenched Mustang.

Trans Am racers were production-based cars with engines of 305 cid or less. Chevy worked a forged steel version of the 283-cid V-8's crankshaft into its 327 V-8 to get 302 cid. Big-port Corvette heads, solid lifters, a hot cam, a baffled oil pan, and a Holley four-barrel on a tuned aluminum manifold were specified. Horsepower was rated at 290.

At least 1000 streetable examples had to be produced, and Chevy's tack was to make the 302 part of a Camaro Regular Production Option Code. So low-key was the effort that the car wasn't advertised, or even mentioned in sales literature. The knowledgeable buyer had to order a base 6-cylinder Camaro ($2466), then scan the order sheet for what turned out to be the most famous RPO in history: Z28.

The package cost $400 and included the 302, the F-41 handling suspension, 15-inch tires on Corvette six-inch Rally wheels, and quick-ratio manual steering. A Muncie four-speed was the only transmission; power front disc brakes were a mandatory $100 option.

RPO Z28 was available on the coupe only and could be combined with the hidden-headlamp RS option group. There were no Z28 emblems on the car, but the package did include broad racing stripes on the hood and trunklid. Camaro's rear lip spoiler was a popular option.

The Z28 had a buckboard ride and sports-car handling. The 302 was a peaky devil, hard to launch and lethargic under 4000 rpm. Driven as it was meant to be, performance was shattering. *Road & Track* settled on 7500 rpm(!) as the optimal shift point and reported 63 mph in first gear, 85 in second, and 113 in third. Top speed approached 140 mph. "If the Z-28 isn't a bona fide racing car," said the magazine, "then we've never seen one."

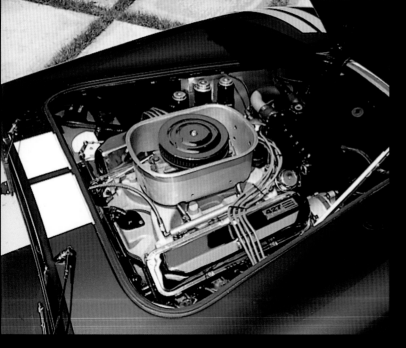

1967 SHELBY
COBRA 427 SC

Perhaps the ultimate in raw sports-car power and performance, the legendary Shelby Cobra 427 has been widely replicated—no surprise, as only 348 originals were built in 1965–67. Though some of the copies have been quite faithful, Carroll Shelby has jealously guarded the car's name and design, even bringing lawsuits against counterfeiters. A few 427s were actually fitted with Ford's low-stress 428 passenger-car V-8, whose gross horsepower is usually quoted as 355. This, however, is a genuine 427, conservatively rated at 390 bhp. Cobras have always thrilled crowds at racetracks. Though they still typically command seven-figure prices as collector cars, they often compete in vintage events, evoking memories of a now-distant sports-car era.

1968
FERRARI
365 GTB/4 DAYTONA

Ferrari unveiled another instant classic in 1968 with the 365 CTB/4, which the press somehow quickly dubbed Daytona. Replacing the 275 CTB/4, it used a similar rear-transaxle chassis and an identical wheelbase but offered even higher performance thanks to a V-12 enlarged from 3.3 to 4.4 liters, which took horsepower from 300 to 352. At just under $20,000, the Daytona was the costliest street Ferrari yet, but also the fastest. *Road & Track* verified the factory's claimed 174-mph top speed and timed the standing quarter-mile in just 13.8 seconds at 107.5 mph. The body design was hailed as one of Pininfarina's best, one reason for the car's long-legendary status. This berlinetta is an early European version with clear headlamp covers. U.S. models initially wore rather warty-looking exposed lights, but all later Daytonas were treated to hidden headlamps in a smooth body-color nose. The Daytona wasn't much changed otherwise, but 1969 introduced a companion spider convertible that's even more sought-after now than the coupe. Designated CTS/4, it saw only 127 copies versus nearly 1300 berlinettas. That was far too few to satisfy demand, which is why some Daytona coupes have since been decapitated to pass as spiders, an important point now for would-be owners—and judges at the ritzy car shows where these Ferraris gather.

1968 FORD GT40

Rebuffed when it tried to buy Ferrari, Ford created the GT40 to exact revenge in international long-distance racing. The basic midengine design originated in Britain but was heavily reworked by Carroll Shelby and other Americans after a troubled 1964 debut season and scant success in '65. Ford reached the pinnacle in 1966 with smashing 1-2-3 finishes at Le Mans and Daytona, thus eclipsing Ferrari at last, then repeated as world manufacturers champion and Le Mans winner in 1967-69. Only 130 racing GT40s were built. Of these, 15 were Mark II versions powered by Ford big-block 427 V-8s prepared by Holman & Moody of stock-car racing fame. The similar-looking Mark I used Ford's 289 small-block V-8, also competition-tuned. There were also a few "Mark III" versions with long-nose bodies, detuned engines, and basic road equipment. This car is one of several Mark II replicas offered in the late 1990s by Holman & Moody scion Lee Holman. Fittingly, it was crafted with original GT40 tooling, which had somehow survived over the years in Britain, where the storied racers were built.

1968
FORD
MUSTANG 428 COBRA JET

Ask the most knowledgeable Ford enthusiasts for the quickest pure-production Mustang ever and rare will be the one who doesn't name the 1968 428 Cobra Jet. Big-block Camaros and Firebirds, and even 340-cid Darts and Barracudas, were kicking Mustang's tail on the street. Ford countered by making its 427-cid V-8 a Mustang option in early '68 models, but it was a detuned 390-bhp version of the legendary near-race 427, and its slim availability and $755 cost were downers.

Then, on April 1, 1968, Ford unreined the Cobra Jet. It was based on the staid 428 big-car engine, but had larger-valve heads, the race-brewed 427 intake manifold, and an oil-pan windage tray. It also had ram-air induction and a functional hood scoop. The scoop mated to a special air cleaner with a vacuum-actuated butterfly valve that funneled air directly into the 735-cfm Holley quad. Output was around 410 bhp, but Ford rated it at 335 bhp in an effort to calm insurance agents and con drag-strip rules-makers.

The 428 CJ was offered in Mustang fastbacks and coupes (and in Torino, Cougar, and Cyclone models) with a four-speed manual or three-speed automatic. Cobra Jet Mustangs had beefed-up front shock towers and Polyglas F70x14 tires. Four-speed cars got staggered rear shocks. Standard were 3.50:1 gears, with 3.91:1 and 4.30:1 ratios available.

CJ Mustangs came with GT-level touches, such as front fog lamps and a side "C" stripe, but the only other external clue to the armament within was the black scoop and hood stripe. The entire package cost about $500, including front disc brakes. The Equa-Loc differential ($79) and Competition Handling Package ($62) were wise extras.

With 11.5-second ETs at 120 mph, Ford's team of eight CJ Mustangs obliterated everything in their Super Stock class at the '68 NHRA Winternationals. The impact was no less forceful on the street. "The entire world will come to recognize this engine—the 428 Cobra Jet—at the pop of a hood," declared *Motor Trend*. Finally, the competition was chasing Mustang's tail.

1968 OLDSMOBILE HURST/OLDS

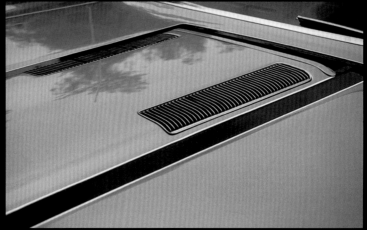

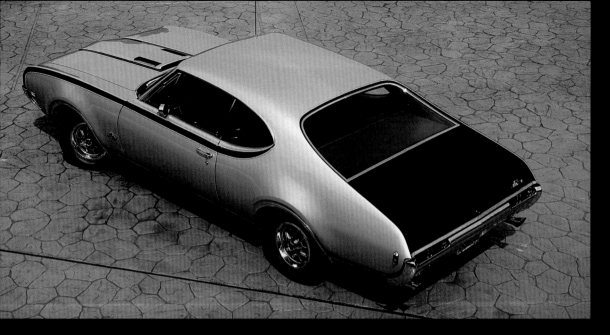

Good thing George Hurst's work was as good as his promotional fervor, because he had a big appetite for attention. By the mid '60s, the former Philadelphia repair-shop owner's name was on some of drag racing's wildest exhibition cars, from the wheelstanding Hemi Under Class to the tire-frying twin-engine Hurst Hairy Olds. And then there was Linda Vaughn, Miss Hurst Golden Shifter....

But for every stunt, there was a good product, like great transmission linkages or Hurst's most important invention, the Jaws of Life rescue tool. It was conservative Oldsmobile, however, that first put the ballyhooed Hurst name on a production car.

The division's 4-4-2 entered '68 with curvaceous new styling courtesy of GM's intermediate-car revamp. Its 400-cid V-8 had 350 bhp—360 with the new Force Air option, a factory-installed induction system that inhaled through scoops beneath the front bumper. The W-30 option returned as a blueprinted 360-bhp mill backed by a beefed-up drivetrain and cost $263.

Hurst engineer Jack "Doc" Watson had built his boss a custom '68 4-4-2. The enterprising Hurst sold Olds on the publicity value of building a limited run of similar cars for sale through key Olds dealers. Whether the Cutlass S coupes Olds shipped to an outside assembly site were already equipped with the special 390-bhp 455-cid Toronado V-8 is under debate, but all the cars did get Force Air systems and Turbo Hydra-Matics with a Hurst Dual-Gate shifter.

The suspension used the best factory components, so handling was on a par with the lauded 4-4-2's. The 455 V-8 was no handicap; it actually weighed 12 pounds less than the 400. All cars were painted Toronado "Peruvian Silver" with black accent stripes and rear-deck panel.

Outstanding power, fuss-free performance, full warranty, and exclusivity came at $1161 over the sticker of a regular 4-4-2. Dealers took 3000 orders for the car, far more than could be filled. The hype was real, and the '68 Hurst/Olds marked the start of a great muscle-car friendship.

1968
PONTIAC
GTO

When GM redesigned its intermediates for '68, no division had a tougher act to follow than Pontiac. But talent rose to the challenge and the new GTO emerged as a brilliant blend of beauty and brawn. It sustained the styling leadership of the 1966–67 series, and its performance remained competitive against ever-tougher rivals. Best of all, its aura was intact.

"In image, performance and class, the 'Tiger' is the car to equal," said *Motor Trend* in its survey of Detroit's '68 muscle armada. "Face it," said *Hot Rod* editors after their first drive in the new Goat, "this is Pontiac's era."

Gone was the pillared coupe, leaving a two-door GTO hardtop and convertible, again with the best dash layout in supercar land. Curb weights were up about 75 pounds over '67, but a wheelbase shortened from 115 inches to a nimbler 112, another year of suspension tuning, and standard G78x14 tires improved handling enough to rival that of the best GM intermediate, the Oldsmobile 4-4-2.

Nothing rivaled the GTO's new energy-absorbing Endura bumper, which was molded and color-keyed to form the car's clean new nose. Hidden headlamps also were new and were so popular that most people didn't realize they were options.

A 400-cid four-barrel V-8 remained standard. The base version gained 15 bhp, to 350, while the HO and Ram Air editions climbed to 360 bhp. Midyear, Pontiac replaced the original Ram Air engine with the Ram Air II. Improvements included new cylinder heads, forged pistons, and lighter valves. Compression was unchanged, but output rose to 366 bhp. The Ram Air induction hardware was again shipped in the trunk for installation by the dealer. All engines were available with Hurst-shifted stick or automatic, though Ram Air cars came only with 4.33:1 gears and without air conditioning.

The steering transmitted too much road shock and had too little feel, and some sheetmetal wasn't the stoutest. But in the increasingly treacherous muscle jungle, the new GTO remained one of the big cats.

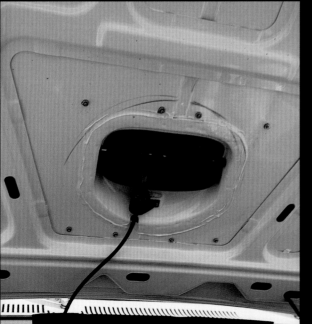

1969
AMC
HURST SC/RAMBLER

Laugh if you will, but the AMC Hurst SC/Rambler could blow the doors off some pedigreed muscle cars. Too bad AMC had to compensate for its slim advertising budget by making a billboard of the car. Having dipped into performance with the '68 AMX and Javelin pony cars, Detroit's No. 4 automaker decided to expand into the budget-muscle arena with—don't snicker—a Rambler Rogue compact. Directed by Hurst Performance Research Inc., the project followed the simplest hot-rod canon: stuff in the biggest available V-8. In AMC's case, that was the AMX's 315-hp 390-cid four-barrel. A Borg-Warner four-speed with a Hurst shifter and a 3.54:1 limited-slip completed the drivetrain.

Heavy-duty shocks, anti-sway bar, and anti-hop rear links fortified the suspension. E70x14 Polyglas tires and the AMC's optional heavy-duty brakes with front discs were included. Inside were reclining buckets. Instrumentation was standard Rogue with the exception of a Sun 8000-rpm tach strapped to the steering column.

The car debuted midway through the model year as the AMC SC/Rambler-Hurst; most called it the Scrambler. Only 1512 were built, and they were potent little screamers. But that exterior treatment! No one seemed to like it. A "tri-colored nickelodeon," said *Car and Driver*.

All SC/Ramblers started as appliance-white hardtops with two-tone mags, racing mirrors, blackout grille and tail panel, Hurst badging, and a real ram-air hood scoop with an upthrust snout that unfortunately recalled the nose of a hound sniffing for the scent. About 1012 Scramblers went full "Yankee Doodle," with broad red bodysides, wild hood graphics, and a fat blue dorsal stripe. The rest made do with only simple rocker-panel striping.

With ETs in the low- to mid-14s, however, some unwary rivals wouldn't have to look at the whole car. "This sort of acceleration," said *Road Test*, "is going to show the Hurst emblem on the back to a few GTOs, Cobra Jets, Road Runners, and Mach 1s."

1969
CHEVROLET
CHEVELLE COPO 427

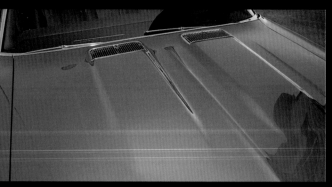

Less flamboyant than Chevelles modified by Chevy performance guru Don Yenko, were the factory COPO Chevelles. These supercars spoke softly, but carried a very big stick.

All COPO Chevelles were cut from the same basic cloth. Their reason for being was GM's ban on engines over 400 cid in midsize cars. Hotbloods within Chevy itched to circumvent the rule. And with a handful of muscle-hungry dealers egging them on, Vince Piggins, Chevy's performance-products manager, found a way. He used the Central Office Production Order system, which normally filled special-equipment fleet orders, to factory-equip a run of Chevelles with L72 427-cid V-8s.

As in the COPO Camaro, the solid-lifter iron-block-and-head L72 used an aluminum manifold and an 800-cfm Holley four-barrel. Chevy rated it at 425 hp, but in calculating the car's stock drag class, the NHRA claimed a truer 450 hp. Chevelle's strongest regular four-speed or the Rock Crusher manual were offered, as was a fortified Turbo Hydra-Matic. The strengthened 12-bolt Positraction axle had 4.10:1 cogs and the suspension was heavy-duty. Front discs—standard on Super Sport Chevelles—were a mandatory $64 option on COPO cars.

In fact, none of the 323 COPO Chevelles built were Super Sports. Instead, they were base coupes with a COPO option package that cost about $860, including $533 for the L72. Yenko put his trademark dress-ups on the 99 he ordered. But the balance that went to other dealers for individual sale looked deceptively docile.

From the SS they borrowed a black grille and tail panel, hood bulges, side stripes, and chrome exhaust tips. However, there was no performance ID on the body. The emblem-free L72 could pass for an aluminum-manifold 396. And the cabin was plain Malibu, though a few SS steering wheels were fitted. Even the standard rally wheels were similar to those on the base Malibu, though they were in reality 15-inch units.

The cid-ceiling would be lifted for '70, so COPO Chevelles were built for 1969 only. But these were among the most feared muscle cars of any day. And they didn't need any badges.

1969
CHEVROLET
NOVA SS 396

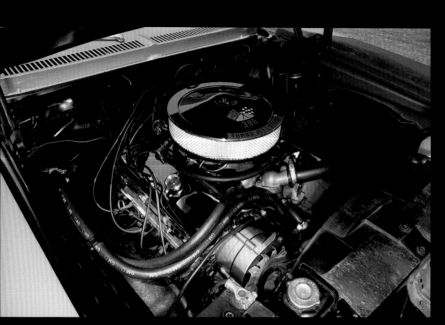

Some street racers weren't attention seekers. They got their kicks by humbling flashy, high-buck muscle cars, shutting them down in an ambush of speed and stealth. The Nova SS 396 seemed ideal for such duty. But looks can be deceiving.

Chevy had redesigned its compact for '68, but the look was still pretty tame. The chassis design, however, was shared with the Camaro, so big blocks finally fit. Sure enough, the 396-cid V-8 appeared as a Super Sport option partway through '68. For '69, the 396 was back in 350-bhp tune and—for those who knew how to play the order form—as the 375-bhp L78.

This was the hoodlum Nova. Building one began with the SS package. It added $280 to the $2405 base price of a Nova pillared coupe and included a 300-bhp 350-cid V-8, special suspension, red stripe F70xl4s, and power front discs. Replacing the 350 with the L78 cost another $500, but even with the $184 close-ratio four-speed, $43 limited-slip, and excellent $84 fast-ratio power steering, the price was an enticing $3500 or so.

SS badges, black-accented grille and tail, and simulated hood air intakes marked the exterior, but nothing shouted supercar. Still, all stealthiness seemed to dissolve with the L78. What the "396" numerals on the fender suggested, the racket of solid lifters and the ominous rumble from dual exhausts confirmed.

"The junior Chevy with the senior engine...is an instantly recognized and feared street cleaner," reported *Car and Driver*. "The 396 Chevy II sure wasn't the invisible sleeper we had expected, but it was every bit as wild as we hoped."

Not only did the SS 396 stuff big power into a 3400-pound package, it put just 55 percent of its heft on the front axle, a favorable weight balance few muscle cars could match. Even so, torque and tire slip conspired to quell bite off the line. Cheater slicks solved the problem. True, they may have given away the Nova SS 396's true mission, but its cover was blown the moment the L78 fired up, anyway.

1969
DODGE
CORONET R/T

With all the hoopla surrounding the arrival of the Super Bee Six Pack and the continued popularity of the Charger, a Dodge original seemed lost in the shuffle. The Coronet R/T was the first Dodge to unify traditional muscle elements under one nameplate back in '67. Sales topped 10,000 for its first two years, but would slide to 7200 for '69, and to 2600 for 1970—the car's swan-song season.

But quantity is not quality, of course, and Dodge continued to fine-tune its gentleman's muscle car for '69. Grille and taillamps were revised and 15-inch aluminum road wheels were optional in place of the standard 14-inchers.

The 375-bhp 440 Magnum four-barrel was again standard. Just 97 hardtops and 10 convertibles were ordered with the sole engine option, the 425-bhp 426 Hemi. A Ramcharger fresh-air induction package that added two sizable hood scoops was a new option with the 440 and was standard with the Hemi, but it didn't alter power ratings.

Dodge had formed the Scat Park to standardize marketing of its performance-car offerings, and now even the R/T's axle ratios were being organized into unified component packages. For example, the drag-oriented Track-Pak grouped a 3.54:1 Dana axle, Sure-Grip differential, dual-point distributor, heavy-duty four-speed with Hurst shifter, and heavy-duty cooling system. Other packages emphasized handling or highway cruising.

On the subject of axle ratios, *Car Life* observed that the 440 Magnum V-8 and three-speed TorqueFlite automatic combination in its Coronet R/T test car was so responsive that the standard 3.23:1 cog could have been replaced with a more economical 2.76:1 axle ratio with little loss of acceleration.

"The 440's brute torque makes high revving completely unnecessary," the magazine said. "Shift points up to 5500 rpm were tried, but 5000 rpm gave the best performance."

Dodge had simplified its hot intermediate to produce the budget-muscle Super Bee, and used its platform for the glamour muscle Charger. In between was the Coronet R/T, a muscle-car original holding—and occasionally dominating—the middle ground.

1969
DODGE
SUPER BEE SIX PACK

In mid-1969, Chrysler engineers used some good-old hot-rodding to create one of the muscle era's most intoxicating cars.

They took Mopar's fine 375-bhp 440-cid Magnum V-8 and treated it to the time-honored hop-up of more carburetion, replacing the single Carter quad with three Holley two-barrels on an Edelbrock Hi-Riser manifold. Normal driving ran the engine on the center carb; punching it opened the two outboard Holleys and delivered an astounding 1375-cfm charge. Hemi valve springs, a hotter cam, magnafluxed connecting rods, and other fortifications helped boost output to 390 bhp.

A Hurst-shifted four-speed and a 93⁄4-inch Dana Sure-Grip diff with 4.10:1 gears were standard. TorqueFlite was optional, but disc brakes, air conditioning, and cruise control were not allowed.

Dodge's home for the new mill was the econo-muscle Coronet Super Bee, which again came with a 383-cid V-8 or the 426 Hemi. In honor of the tri-carb setup, the newcomer was called the Super Bee Six Pack, a name broadcast on the sides of one of the wilder hoods in muscledom. Its scoop lacked a filter or valve to keep out foreign elements—though it did have rain drain tubes. With its matte-black finish and NASCAR tie-down pins, the fiberglass lift-off hood said this car meant business, a message reinforced by standard steel wheels unadorned except for chrome lug nuts. (The engine and a similar hood also were offered in the '69 Plymouth Road Runner as the "440+6".)

Dodge's 440 Six Pack cost $463, about $500 less than a Hemi. No Mopar mill was as all-out fast as the Hemi. But the 440 could hang with one until 70 mph or so, and the deep-breathing Six Pack added a near-Hemi high end. "The result was a torque motor that would rev, too, a fearsome street cleaner," wrote *Car and Driver's* Patrick Bedard in his 1990 muscle retrospective.

With their Hemi-grade suspension, Six Pack Super Bees were surprisingly good handlers. That outrageous hood did bait cops, and made every oil check a two-person job. So what? Considering its price and performance, this Six Pack was a small-deposit, high-return steal.

1969
FORD
MUSTANG MACH 1 428 COBRA JET

Ford's fight to shed its also-ran image got a boost when the Mach I moved into the starting gate. Here was a Mustang that looked the part of a modern muscle pony, and with the 428 Cobra Jet, it ran like one.

Mustang was restyled for '69, gaining 3.8 inches of body length—all ahead of the front wheels— and about 140 pounds of curb weight. The flowing lines looked right in new Mach I livery. This was the mainstream performance version. It came standard with a 351-cid V-8, but star of the stable was the optional 428-cid Cobra Jet. Essentially the same V-8 that put Ford muscle on the map in the 1968 1/2 Cobra Jet Mustang, it came in three states of tune for '69. The base version without Ram Air cost $224; $133 more bought the fresh-air induction system, which this year used a new "shaker" hood in which a scoop mounted to the air cleaner protruded through a hole in the hood and vibrated ominously with the engine.

A third version triggered by the $155 Drag-Pack option was the 428 Super Cobra Jet Ram Air. It used the shaker scoop, plus a modified crankshaft and stronger connecting rods for better high-rpm durability, as well as an engine oil cooler that decreased lubricant temperature by 30 degrees. The Drag Pack came with limited-slip 3.91:1 or 4.30:1 cogs and excluded air conditioning. All versions used a four-speed or Ford's improved SelectShift automatic. And all were underrated at 335 bhp. But the Cobra Jet's most-pertinent product was torque, enough to send the F40x14s up in a haze of Polyglas. With 3.91:1 gearing, even the automatic broke 'em loose at each full-throttle upshift. Great for grins, bad for ETs. The root of the problem was a 59-percent front-weight bias, an imbalance that contributed to sloppy handling, as well.

But this was the Mustang Ford fans had waited for—cheaper than a Boss 429, less temperamental than a Boss 302, and a force anywhere fast cars gathered.

1969
CHEVROLET
YENKO CAMARO 427

To Ford fans, Carroll Shelby is the high priest of performance. Chevy loyalists revere a Canonsburg, Pennsylvania, car dealer named Don Yenko. Yenko had a deserved reputation for driving, building, and selling dominating Chevrolets, starting in '65 with well-crafted super Corvairs. He advanced to installing 427-cid Corvette V-8s in '67 and '68 Camaros, performing 118 of the transplants. These $4200 ponys ran in the low 13s right off his shop floor.

Other Chevy retailers, notably Nickey in Chicago, Dana in California, and Baldwin-Motion in New York, undertook similar transplants. But Yenko Sports Cars Inc. had dealer outlets for its cars in 19 states, and that earned clout with Chevrolet. Dealer conversions were complicated, however, and came with only a limited engine warranty. So at Yenko's urging, Chevy agreed to factory build a batch of 1969 Camaros with 427 engines, and to provide full five-year/50,000-mile warranties. This was done under the Central Office Production Order system, which had previously been used to satisfy special requests from nonperformance fleet buyers.

How many COPO Camaros were built isn't known; Yenko ordered 201, but other dealers could order them as well, and 500 or more were produced. All were basically the same: They had the iron-block and head, solid-lifter L72 427, which Chevy pegged at 425 bhp but which Yenko rated a more realistic 450; Hurst four-speed manual or Dual-Cate automatic; heavy-duty 4.10:1 Posi; cowl-induction hood; heavy-duty Z28 suspension with F70x14 tires; and other go-fast goodies. The package added about $800 to a base coupe, including $490 for the engine.

Chevy delivered the standard COPO Camaros with dog-dish hubcaps and no exterior badging; not even the engine was identified as a 427. Yenko ordered his with 15-inch rally wheels, bigger front roll bar, and 140-mph speedometer, then dressed them with "sYc" (Yenko Super Car) insignia and striping, and made available mags, gauges, headers, and other items that could push the price past $4600. As delivered, Yenko Camaros turned effortless mid-13s. Most were fitted with headers and slicks, even for street work, and in this form recorded 11.94-second ETs at 114 mph.

AMC
AMX

derived from the Javelin pony car, with shared mechanicals, seats, and dashboard. To purists who debated whether even the 'Vette was a true sports car, a shortened Javelin wasn't worth discussing.

To most Americans, of course, the fact that the AMX wasn't an MG was an advantage. That meant it was reasonably comfortable, had lots of luggage space, and most importantly, could be equipped with a big, powerful V-8 engine.

After bowing midway through the '68 model year, the AMX was largely unaltered for '69, though a Hurst shifter did replace its inferior factory linkage. Changes were more substantial for '70.

Standard in place of a 225-bhp 290-cid V-8 was a new 290-bhp 360. The optional 390 V-8 got freer-flowing heads and other improvements that gave it a 10-bhp boost, to 325. The restyled hood carried a scoop that was made functional when the new Ram Air option was ordered. AMC also moved the parking/turn-signal lamps to the grille, creating holes in the bumper that it said cooled the front brakes. Actually, the ducts were too far from the binders to do much good. More effective was a revised front suspension that further improved the already sharp handling.

Optimally set up with the $384 "Co" package, which included E70x14 tires, front disc brakes, super heavy-duty suspension, limited-slip diff, Ram Air, and improved engine cooling, a 390 AMX was reasonably quick in the quarter and highly competent in the corners. It was a rewarding combination, and so rare in a car from Detroit that some testers were not about to quibble over the sports-car label.

"For the doubters we can testify once again that the AMX feels like a sports car, drives like a sports car, handles like a sports car and therefore in our book (and that of the Sports Car Club of America) it is a sports car," said *Road Test* magazine.

But this, the best AMX, was also the last true AMX. For '71, the proud AMX lost its identity as a short-wheelbase two-seater and reverted to a decor option for the redesigned and horribly bloated four-seat Javelin.

DODGE
CHALLENGER T/A

When Dodge finally got a legitimate pony car to race in the Sports Car Club of America's Trans American Sedan Championship, it built a version for the street that went the competition car one wilder.

SCCA rules required Dodge to sell production editions of the track car, and Dodge responded with the Challenger T/A. The race cars ran a destroked 305-cid version of Mopar's fine 340-cid V-8. It had a four-barrel carb and some 440 bhp. Street T/As stayed with the 340, but upped the ante with a trio of two-barrel Holleys atop an Edelbrock aluminum intake manifold. Despite the "Six Pak" carburetion and a host of internal reinforcements, the T/A's mill carried the same 290 bhp rating as regular four-barrel 340s, though true output was near 350 bhp. Feeding it air was a suitcase-size scoop molded into the matte-black fiberglass hood. Low-restriction dual exhausts ran to the stock muffler location under the trunk, then reversed direction to exit in chrome-tipped "megaphone" outlets in front of the rear wheels.

TorqueFlite automatic or Hurst-shifted four-speed, 3.55:I or 3.90:I gears, manual or power steering were available. Front discs were standard. The special Rallye suspension used heavy-duty everything and increased the camber of the rear springs. The T/A was among the first production cars with different size tires front and rear: E60xI5s up front, G60xI5s in back. The modified camber elevated the tail enough to clear the rear rubber and the exhaust outlets, giving the T/A a real street-punk's stance. Thick side stripes, bold ID graphics, and a black ducktail spoiler joined the visual assault, though the cabin was standard Challenger R/T.

As it turned out, the T/A wasn't a consistent SCCA winner, and its street sibling didn't act much like a road racer, succumbing to debilitating understeer in fast corners. But the intensified 340 and meaty rear tires helped production versions claw through the quarter in the mid-I4s, a showing that would do any small-block pony proud.

1970
DODGE
CHARGER R/T HEMI

Like a veteran heavyweight calling on all his tools to finish strong in the late rounds, the Charger R/T returned for the last year of its classic period with an unprecedented array of tricks.

A new chrome loop front bumper was echoed by a fresh full-width taillamp housing, and R/T versions gained a simulated reverse body-side scoop. The color palette took on a younger look, borrowing high-impact hues like Plum Crazy and Go-Mango from the new Challenger. New front seats were the car's first to qualify as true buckets, and a hip pistol-grip handle now topped the available four-speed's Hurst shifter. Carried over was the extra-cost SE (Special Edition) group with its leather upholstery. And for the first time, Charger could be optioned with an electric sliding sunroof.

Again standard on the R/T was the 375-bhp 440-cid four-barrel, but for those who didn't wish to shell out another $648 for the 425-bhp 426 Hemi, there was a new choice, the 390-bhp 440 with a trio of Holley two-barrels. Its cost and upkeep were friendlier than the Hemi's, torque was identical (at 800 less rpm), and in a street fight few big cars were tougher than a 440 Six Pack. King Kong itself grew more accommodating with the addition of hydraulic lifters, which were better than solid tappets at maintaining the valve lash so essential for good Hemi performance. Still, being fast with a Hemi required keeping all eight carburetor barrels from opening until the tires hooked up. Not every driver was so skillful. "If you were Hemi hunting in a lesser car, you wanted to catch him at a stop," explained Patrick Bedard in his 1990 *Car and Driver* "street warriors" retrospective. "If he fumbled and you were lucky enough to pull out a fender-length on him, you claimed victory early by backing off the power, thereby ending the run. If you were crazy enough to stay on it, the Hemi would take over in short order."

No Charger offered a broader array of thrills and frills than the '70. But rising insurance rates and tougher competition caused R/T sales to fall 50 percent, to 10,337, for the model year. With 116 orders, the new Six Pack outsold the Hemi by more than two to one.

If Ford was embarrassed that its finest Mustangs were the handiwork of the same guys who developed the best Camaros, it certainly never said so. Revenge is sweet. GM executive Semon "Bunkie" Knudsen, who used performance to revive Pontiac, defected to become president of Ford in 1968. He brought along stylist Larry Shinoda, whose work included the Z28 that had unseated Mustang as '68 and '69 Trans Am champ. The Mach I was among their first efforts, but the most special '69 and '70 Mustangs drew on Shinoda's nickname for Knudsen, "boss."

Like the Z28, the Boss 302 was built as a Trans Am road-racing qualifier. Its heart was Ford's 302-cid V-8 treated to the high-performance, big-port cylinder heads being readied for the famous Cleveland 351. The Boss's solid-lifter small-block used the biggest carb employed by Ford, a 780-cfm Holley four-barrel, and was underrated at the same 290 bhp as the Z28's 302. A Hurst-shifted four speed and 3.50:1 gears were standard; 3.91:1 and Detroit Locker 4.30:1 cogs were optional. Underneath were racing-inspired suspension modifications, Polyglas F60xl5s, and power front discs.

Shinoda's expertise in aerodynamics influenced the Boss's exterior. Mustang's phony fender vents were enclosed and a front spoiler was fitted; a rear air foil and backlight blinds were optional. Blackout trim and stripes finished the look. Ford built 1628 Boss 302s for '69, then came back with 7013 for '70, when quad headlamps were traded for double units flanked by fake air intakes, a "shaker" hood scoop was made available, and the engine got smaller intake valves and a 6000-rpm rev limiter.

In Trans Am, racing Boss 302s retook the '70 crown from Chevy. Street versions weren't always as fast as a 302 Z28, but they had more cornering power and a less-peaky, more flexible engine. "The Boss 302 is a hell of an enthusiast's car," said *Car and Driver.* "It's what the Shelby GT 350s and 500s should have been but weren't."

1970
PLYMOUTH
AAR 'CUDA

Of course, the production AAR 'Cuda couldn't be mechanically identical to its Trans Am racing namesake. But unlike the Mustang Boss 302 and Camaro Z28, which also were built to homologate track cars, it didn't even try to mimic the pavement-hugging posture of its competition cousin. What Plymouth built was a street rod.

The AAR 'Cuda took its title from Dan Gurney's All-American Racers, the team that campaigned Barracudas in the Sports Car Club of America's popular competition series. Like the similar racing Dodge Challenger T/As, track AARs ran full-race 440-bhp 305-cid four-barrel V-8s and were lowered and modified for all-out twisty-course combat. And like production Challenger T/As built to qualify the cars for racing, street AARs used a 290-bhp 340-cid with three two-barrel Holley carbs on an Edelbrock aluminum manifold. Buyers could choose a four-speed or TorqueFlite, with a Sure-Grip axle and standard 3.55:1 or optional 3.91:1 gears. The engine breathed through a functional hood scoop.

The AAR's interior was basic 'Cuda, but its exterior certainly was not. From a matte-black fiberglass hood, through body-side strobe stripes and tri-colored AAR shield, to the standard black ducktail spoiler, this was an exotic fish. Special shocks and recambered rear springs raised the tail 1¾ inches over regular 'Cuda specs, allowing clearance for exhaust pipes that exited in front of the rear wheelwell (after routing through the standard muffler beneath the trunk). It also permitted use of C60x15 tires in back and E60x15s in front.

With its raked stance, oversize rear rubber, side-exit exhausts, and loud graphics, an AAR was better suited to a Saturday night at Burger King than a Sunday afternoon at Lime Rock. With a 56 percent front weight bias, handling was plagued by understeer, prompting *Car and Driver* to suggest "it might have been better to put the fat tires on the front wheels." But the AAR 'Cuda was strong in a straight line, and an eyeful anywhere. Just like a good street rod.

1970
PLYMOUTH
ROAD RUNNER SUPERBIRD

Aerodynamic testing began to come into its own in automotive design in the late Sixties. Cars of all sorts benefited, but few had the visual drama of the Plymouth Road Runner Superbird.

Like the similar '69 Dodge Charger Daytona, the Superbird was a "homologation special": In order to be eligible to run in NASCAR events in 1970, a given model's production run had to equal half the number of the manufacturer's dealers, or 1000 cars, whichever figure was higher. Ultimately, 1920 Superbirds were made and offered for sale at steep prices that began at $4298.

The metal front-nose clip, with chin spoiler and fiberglass tubs for pop-up headlamps, was fitted to front fenders and a lengthened hood borrowed from the '70 Dodge Coronet. Other aerodynamic parts—including the car's towering aluminum wing—were developed expressly for the Belvedere/Road Runner body, and thus were not related to similar pieces of the Charger Daytona.

Unique, too, of course, were the Warner Bros. Road Runner graphics, which gave this very serious competition car a nice touch of whimsy.

All production Superbirds wore vinyl tops that hid the weld seams left by installation of the flush-mounted back window. As on the Charger Daytona, rearward-facing scoops on the front fenders were nonfunctional on production Superbirds but allowed the fender tops to be cut for tire clearance and suspension travel on competition cars.

Three engines were offered: a 375-horsepower 440 with a single four-barrel carburetor; the 390-horse 440 Six Pack with triple two-barrel carbs; or the 425-horse 426 Hemi, with a 10.25:1 compression ratio.

In competition trim, the Superbird could top 220 mph; at the 1970 Daytona 500, Pete Hamilton beat the field with an average speed of 150 mph. The Superbird went on to take 21 of 38 Grand National events that year.

1970
PONTIAC
FIREBIRD TRANS AM

Firebird and Camaro grew more European in nature with their second-generation redesign, but the scooped and spoilered Trans Am was pure American muscle, and more immodest than ever.

Its standard V-8, the 345-bhp Ram Air 400-cid, furnished low-14-second ETs. That apparently satisfied most buyers, because just 88 of 3196 Trans Ams built for '70 got the optional Ram Air IV. That one added bigger ports, better heads, swirl-polished valves, and an aluminum intake manifold, for 370 bhp, 25 more than in '69. Rarer still was the Ram Air V, an over-the-counter, special-order piece that counted among its tricks solid lifters and tunnel-port heads for as much as 500 bhp. All these engines breathed through a new rear-facing shaker scoop designed to capture cool ambient air flowing over the hood. A four-speed with Hurst shifter was standard, and a Turbo Hydra-Matic was optional. Both came with 3.55:1 gears, and a 3.73:1 was available with the four-speed.

Road manners received much attention. The padded Formula steering wheel directed quick 12.1:1 variable-ratio power steering. Stiffer springs and heavy-duty front and rear sway bars teamed with Polyglas F60x15 tires on Rally II wheels. Standard 10.9-inch power front disc brakes and 9.5-inch rear drums did the stopping.

Trans Am wore the same impact-absorbing snout as other Firebirds, but Pontiac said its unique front air dam and fender air extractors created 50 pounds of downforce on the nose at expressway speeds. It claimed equal downforce to the tail from a big decklid lip and small spoilers in front of the rear wheels. Inside, complete instrumentation was standard and included a tachometer turned on its side to redline at 12 o'clock, just like in a real race car.

Critics were impressed. Even with 57 percent of the weight on the front wheels, *Sports Car Graphic* said, "Overall handling feel—for a production car—was as near to a front engine race car as we have ever driven." And *Car and Driver* called the '70 Trans Am "a hard muscled, lightning-reflexed commando of a car, the likes of which doesn't exist

1971

CHEVROLET
CHEVELLE SS 454

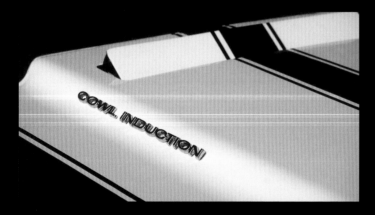

Quarter-mile times in the low-14s required no apology, but they weren't too impressive coming off a year in which the best Chevelles dipped into the low 13s. Chevrolet, like all of Detroit, was struggling to cope with a world that had changed overnight.

Emissions standards had forced a switch to low-lead fuel, which in turn cut compression ratios, while insurance surcharges on supercars prompted tamer horsepower-to-weight ratios. The impact was obvious in the 1971 Chevelle SS line, where small-blocks re-emerged in the form of two 350-cid V-8s: a 245-bhp two-barrel and a 270-bhp four-barrel.

But big-block power still was available. The 402-cid four-barrel cost $173 and had 300 hp, 50 hp below the previous year's base SS engine. To retain the hallowed SS 396 badging, Chevy had called the 1970 402 a "396." For '71, it was renamed the "Turbo Jet 400."

Chevy had taunted enthusiasts with word that the majestic 454-cid LS6 would be back for '71. Compression would be a modest 9.0:1, but output a still-formidable 425 bhp. It was never released for public sale, however. Instead, the hydraulic-lifter LS5 returned as a $279 option on top of the basic SS package. Compression fell to 8.5:1, from 10.25:1, but hp actually increased by five to 365, though it peaked 600 rpm lower than in '70. Torque was down by 35 lb-ft. The LS5 was teamed with the Turbo Hydra-Matic 400 or the M22 Rock Crusher four-speed; 3.31:1 gears were standard, with a 4.10:1 Posi optional.

The basic SS package included a lot for its $357 price: the F41 suspension with front and rear stabilizer bars, power front discs, wider F60 tires on larger 15-inch five-spoke wheels, and blackout grille. All Chevelles got single headlamps, and the SS could be spiffed with optional racing stripes and the extra-cost cowl induction hood. Interestingly, only LS5 cars carried external engine ID; their badges said "SS 454." All others wore simple "SS" insignia. That was a pretty revealing sign of the times.

1971
DODGE
CHARGER R/T HEMI

With muscle in retreat, the last thing anyone would have expected to see on the order sheet was the 426 Hemi, but there it was. Granted, not many were delivered for '71, but that didn't mean the Hemi didn't still deliver.

Mopar was holding out better than most against the anti-performance onslaught. Compression ratios were down only fractionally, and horsepower cuts were not severe. The Hemi continued with a 10.25:1 squeeze and retained 425 bhp and 490 lb-ft of torque. Chrysler installed just 356 of the mills for '71, 186 of them in Dodge Challengers and Plymouth 'Cudas.

The balance was spread among the redesigned Plymouth Road Runner and GTX, and the new Dodge Charger and its close cousin, the Charger Super Bee. The '71 Charger was a radical departure from its predecessor, losing two inches of wheelbase and gaining swoopy Coke-bottle contours. It now shared its body with the Super Bee, and though its performance leader retained the R/T designation, the only '71 Charger to come standard with the car's trademark hidden headlamps was the luxury SE version; they were otherwise optional.

But the R/T stayed true to its roots with a daunting underhood lineup. The 370-bhp 440-cid four-barrel Magnum V-8 was standard, with the 385-bhp 440 Six Pack available at extra cost. Topping the roster was the Hemi, which cost $884, not including required extras such as the Sure-Grip diff. A four-speed was standard, TorqueFlite was optional, and Hemi Chargers fed their dual quads with an Air Grabber-type hood scoop activated by a dashboard switch.

A standard blackout hood, faux bodyside air extractors, Rallye wheels, tape stripes, and optional front and rear spoilers made this the most garish Charger ever, particularly when swathed in extra-cost colors like "Hemi Orange" and "Citron Yella." Charger retained this body style through 1974, but would never again have a Hemi. Chrysler dropped the engine from the roster after this year, making 1971 the requiem for this heavyweight.

1972
LAMBORGHINI
MIURA SV

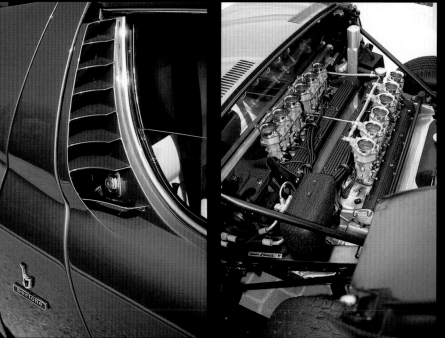

The Lamborghini Miura had been improving in stages since its 1966 debut. The last and fastest iteration of the iconic mid-V-12 coupe was the P400SV, appearing in 1971. Against the previous Miura S, it packed 15 extra horsepower—385 total—thanks to more changes in cam timing and carburetors, plus bigger valves. Other alterations included a larger fuel tank, more effective engine oiling, vented brake rotors (versus solid), and revised rear suspension geometry that raised ride height slightly but improved handling in concert with another upsizing of wheels and tires. The cockpit wasn't ignored either, as switchgear, instruments, and trim were either upgraded, remodeled, or both. The wild Marcello Gandini styling still looked great even after six years and wisely wasn't changed much. However, the SV did get visibly wider rear flanks (to accommodate the broader tires), a discreet ID badge on the tail, and layback headlamps without the surrounding "eyelash" trim that had caused a few giggles on earlier Miuras. With top speed up to 175 mph and acceleration to match, the SV was faster than a Ferrari Daytona and most any other street-legal machine. But Lamborghini was readying an even more outrageous supercar, so the Miura said goodbye in January 1973 when the last SV was sold. Ironically, an unprecedented world energy crisis hit just nine months later, that, at the time, seemed to spell the end for all high-power "exoticars." Fortunately, that pessimistic view would prove to be quite inaccurate.

1973
PORSCHE
911 CARRERA RS

Built for Group 4 GT racing and reviving a historic Porsche name, the 1973 Carrera RS boasted a new 230-bhp 2.7-liter flat six, beefed-up chassis, and lightweight coupe bodywork with broader fender flares, bold bodyside graphics, and a distinctive "ducktail" rear spoiler. Porsche ran off 1636 RS 2.7s, mainly for Europe, where the model was street legal. A few came to America, but a "dirty" engine meant owners couldn't drive them except on a racetrack.

1975 LAMBORGHINI
LP400 COUNTACH

Unveiled as a concept in 1971, the midengine Lamborghini Countach was no less astonishing when sales began in '74. Replacing the Miura, the new LP400 transferred the familiar 5.0-liter twincam V-12 to a waist-high Bertone-designed coupe with "scissor" doors and 98.4-inch wheelbase. It was cramped, stiff-riding, and tough to see out of, but who cared? The Countach was Batmobile cool and bat-outta-hell quick, capable of 175 mph and 0-60 mph in well under 7 seconds. In 1978 came the LP400S with flared fenders, ultrawide wheels and tires, front spoiler, and refinements to suspension and cockpit. It wasn't any faster, but it was somewhat easier to drive in traffic—if you had to. Alas, few Americans got the chance, and then mainly through "gray market" channels, as Lamborghini's mounting financial troubles prevented it from meeting all U.S. standards, thus largely precluding factory sales. That only made the Countach even more the dream ride for "bad boys" with connections and over $50,000 to burn.

1990
CHEVROLET
CORVETTE ZR1

Rumors about it had circulated for years, and by late 1989 it was ready: the ZRI. Actually a $27,000 option for the $32,000 1990 Corvette coupe, the ZRI extended the Corvette credo of world-class performance at middle-class prices to a new level. Fans called it King of the Hill, and some paid $100,000 for the first examples off the assembly line—then put them in storage. The ZRI's Ferrari-like performance helped give CM a needed image boost, though its only visual distinction from other 'Vettes was squared-off taillamps set into a wider, convex tail, a design needed to accommodate its wider rear tires. The FX3 adjustable suspension with touring, sport, and performance settings was standard. The ZRI arrived with a revamped interior that introduced a driver-side airbag, a design common to all '90 Corvettes. A showcase of powertrain technology, the ZRI would be offered through 1995, and a total of 6939 were produced.

After considering a variety of homegrown turbo powerplants, Chevy got Britain's Lotus to design a sophisticated naturally aspirated V-8. Dubbed the LT5 and built by Mercury Marine in Oklahoma, the all-alloy dohc 32-valve 5.7-liter V-8 had 375 horsepower and came with a console-mounted "valet key" that cut power to about 210 bhp. It propelled the 3500-pound coupe from 0-60 mph in 4.5 seconds, through the quarter-mile in 12.4 at 111 mph, and to a top speed of 175. Plus, it averaged 17 mpg city/26 highway. A six-speed manual was the only available transmission. Horsepower would rise to 405 for 1993. ZRI showed America could produce world-class performance and helped propel the sports car into a new golden age.

1990 LAMBORGHINI
DIABLO

True to tradition, Lamborghini's supercar for the Nineties was named for a fighting bull, but Diablo is another word for devil. Indeed, it certainly had enough power to feel possessed. Lamborghini engineers succeeded in the formidable task of creating a new car that one-upped the Countach while retaining its heritage and meeting modern-day safety and emissions standards. The Diablo was the only Lamborghini developed under Chrysler, which furnished computer-design expertise and also softened the lines of designer Marcello Candini's original styling. The 492-bhp, 5.7-liter V-12's performance was appropriately ferocious, with 4.5-second 0-60 mph times and a 202-mph top speed. By 1996, the Diablo line had expanded to include the all-wheel-drive VT roadster, the lightweight SV with flashy body-side graphics, and the race-ready SVR.

1992 DODGE
VIPER

Chrysler revived the spirit of the hallowed 1960s Shelby Cobra 427SC with the milestone Dodge Viper RT/10. After a show-stopping concept debut at the 1989 Detroit Auto Show and a whirlwind development cycle, production Vipers were

1992
JAGUAR
XJ220

The Jaguar XJ220 drew much praise—and collected more than 1000 order deposits—when it was first shown in 1988 as a concept vehicle. That original XJ220 concept boasted a V-12 engine and projected top speed of 220 mph, but much had changed by the time the car went on sale in 1992 as a production model. The V-12 was replaced by a 540-horsepower 3.5-liter V-6 version of the engine that powered Jaguar racecars, and all-wheel drive was replaced by rear-wheel drive. A production XJ220 was timed at 217.1 mph—not quite 220, but fast enough to take the Guinness World Record as the fastest standard production car. The 0-60 mph time was a blistering 3.6 seconds. In spite of the XJ220's high performance, sales were disappointing—only 271 examples were built. Many potential buyers didn't like the substitution of a V-6 engine, and an early-Nineties recession significantly hampered the supercar market.

1994 ASTON MARTIN DB7

Introduced in Europe in 1994 and the U.S. in 1996, the DB7 was the first Aston Martin developed under Ford Motor Company, which took control of Aston in 1987. Aston Martin wisely revived the DB name, which had been dropped in 1972, for this model. Ford money helped develop, test, and certify the car, but the DB7 was designed by Aston to be an Aston. Available in both coupe and Volante convertible versions, the voluptuous body was styled by Aston's Ian Callum, formerly of Ford's Chia studio, with subtle nods to DBs of the past. A refined dohc inline-six put out 335 bhp with the help of an Eaton supercharger and propelled the DB7 to 5.5-second 0-60 mph times and a 165-mph top speed when equipped

Sumptuous interiors featured Connolly hide upholstery, deep-pile carpet, and burr walnut dashboard and console trim. Production of under 700 cars per year guaranteed exclusivity, as did the $125,000 sticker price. A top-line DB7 Vantage was introduced for 1999. Its 6.0-liter V-12 put out 420 bhp and was good for top speeds of over 180 mph. Although underwritten by Ford, these cars represented the summit of British automaking.

1996
MCLAREN
F1

Drawing on multiple Formula I, CanAm, and Indianapolis victories, England's McLaren organization set about creating its first road car in 1989. Revealed to the public in 1992, the McLaren FI was on the road by 1994 and in the winner's circle at Le Mans in 1995. With its no-holds-barred engineering, the FI redefined the term "supercar." Scissor-type doors provided access to a leather interior with an unusual "1+2" layout: a form-fitting driver seat was centrally located, with a passenger seat slightly aft on both sides. A BMW-designed 6.I-liter V-12 was mounted amidships and packed 627 bhp. A carbon-fiber body/chassis structure made for an unprecedented power-to-weight ratio of under four lbs per horsepower. Price and performance were equally stratospheric: $810,000, 0-60 mph in 3.2 seconds, II.I-second quarter-mile times, and a 231-mph top speed.; 95 mph was possible in second gear. When production ceased in 1997, only 100 cars, including CTR and Le Mans competition versions, had been built.

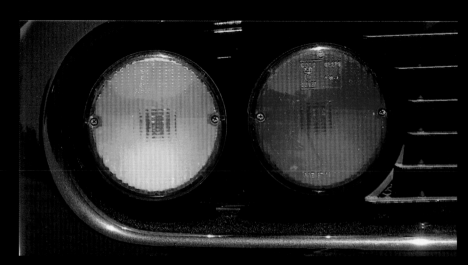

2001
CHEVROLET
CORVETTE Z06

Replacing the short-lived hardtop in the Corvette lineup, the Z06 became the ultimate expression of Chevrolet's long-lived sports car. Introduced in 2001, the Z06 featured the firmest suspension in the 'Vette stable and a breathed-on version of the standard 5.7-liter V-8, good for 385 horsepower. Power jumped to 405 bhp for 2002. The bargain of the supercar crowd, the $53,000 Z06 was clocked reaching 60 mph in 4.5 seconds by *Road & Track*, on par with Ferrari's $170,000 Modena. Visible here are the red calipers of the Z06's enhanced brakes. With an all-new "C6" Corvette due for 2005, Chevrolet dropped the Z06 after 2004, planning to replace it with an even higher-performance version by 2006.

2002
LAMBORGHINI
MURCIELAGO

Next in line to carry the Lamborghini's supercar torch, Murciélago took over where the Diablo left off. New for 2002, a roadster joined the line in 2004. Though Murciélago means "bat" in Spanish, the stealthy implications of the name were lost on these cars. The beefy Lambo V-12 returned for Murciélago duty, enlarged to 6.2 liters, up from the Diablo's 6.0. Producing a prodigious 575 bhp, the Italian sports car reached 60 mph in a scant 3.7 seconds, according to *Motor Trend.* Top speed was in excess of 200 mph. Rare among exotics, Murciélago put power to the ground through a full-time all-wheel-drive system. Murciélago prices started at $280,000.

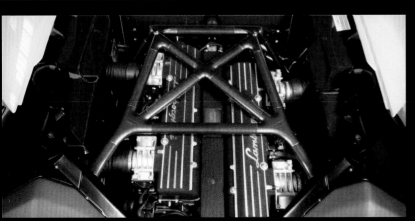

2003-04
FERRARI
ENZO

The crown jewel of the Ferrari lineup, the limited-production Enzo came and went in the blink of an eye. Applying the company's famous "demand minus one" formula, Ferrari built just 399 of the stunning coupes—all in 2003 and 2004. Extracting 660 horsepower from a 6.0-liter midship-mounted V-12, and weighing less than 3000 pounds, performance was eye-popping. According to *Road & Track* magazine, the Enzo sprang from 0-60 mph in a scant 3.3 seconds, and topped out at nearly 220 mph. Equally breathtaking was the Enzo's price, about $650,000. The only available transmission was a 6-speed clutchless "sequential" manual unit with steering-wheel-mounted paddle shifters. Extensive use of exotic materials helped make Ferrari's lithe dancer the welterweight it was. Body panels were formed of a carbon fiber and Nomex "sandwich," while the chassis and tub were formed of carbon fiber. Named for the company's founder who died in August 1988, the car's official name was Ferrari Enzo Ferrari, but fans and the press quickly reduced it to simply Enzo. Color choices were limited to yellow, black, and Ferrari's trademark red. Guaranteeing the Enzo's rarity stateside, Ferrari shipped only 100 cars to America.

Bearing a name synonymous with sports cars, Porsche was not about to be left out of the supercar renaissance. The stunning Carrera GT arrived on the scene for 2004, and moved promptly to the head of the Porsche class. The GT boasted Porsche's largest ever street-going engine, a 5.7-liter V-10. With 605 bhp on tap, the midship-mounted-engine moved the 3000-pound GT to 60 mph in a factory-claimed 3.9 seconds. Top speed was reported to be in excess of 200 mph. To make the most of the car's limited storage space, Porsche included a matching five-piece luggage set with each car. Price: just under $400,000.

2004
PORSCHE
CARRERA GT

2005
BUGATTI
VEYRON

Bugatti's twenty-first century renaissance began with Veyron and its promised 1001-horsepower V-16. Federalized models actually delivered 987 horsepower, roughly double Viper's power output. Production began for 2005, and was limited to 50 vehicles annually. Now under Volkswagen control, the latest Bugatti revival was free of the financial limitations that killed a 1990s rebirth effort.

2015
CHEVROLET
CORVETTE Z06

The C7-generation Chevrolet Corvette that arrived in 2014 was significantly lighter and stiffer than the C6 Corvette it replaced. A new "King of the Hill" version came one year later with the revival of the super-performance Z06 model. The C7 Z06 had a supercharged 6.2-liter V-8 with 650 horsepower and 650 pound-feet of torque, which enabled it to accelerate from 0-60 mph in 3.2 seconds with the 7-speed manual transmission, or a jaw-dropping 2.95 seconds with the 8-speed automatic. *Road & Track* achieved a top speed of 186 mph. In spite of its incredible performance, the Z06 was surprisingly livable in everyday driving. Plus, the base price began at under $80,000—a fraction of the cost of other supercars with comparable capabilities.

2016
LAMBORGHINI
AVENTADOR S

Ferruccio Lamborghini chose a charging bull as the emblem for his car company, and had a tradition of naming models after famous fighting bulls. That practice continued under the Lamborghini firm's various corporate owners over the years—the Aventador, which debuted as a 2011 model, was named for a fighting bull from the Nineties. For 2016, an Aventador S version was introduced; it featured a more sophisticated suspension and a four-wheel steering system that allowed sharper steering at low speeds and better stability at high speeds. There was also a more powerful 740-horsepower 6.5-liter V-12 that could push the all-wheel- drive, mid-engine supercar to 217 mph, with 0-62 mph coming in just 2.9 seconds. The S's base price was around $450,000.

2017 BUGATTI
CHIRON

There are supercars, and then there are supercars, and the Bugatti Chiron definitely qualifies as the latter. The Chiron's quad-turbocharged 8.0-liter W-16 engine developed an astonishing 1500 horsepower and 1180 pound-feet of torque—enough for a 0-60 mph time of 2.4 seconds and an electronically limited top speed of 261 mph. A Haldex all-wheel- drive system got all that power to the road with the least amount of drama. The Chiron set a world record by accelerating 0 to 400 km/h (248 mph) and then braking to a stop in 41.96 seconds. That record was quickly bettered by Koenigsegg, but it was still a remarkable accomplishment. Base price for the Chiron was around $3,000,000. As expected at that price, there was no visible plastic in the cockpit—only top-grade leather and metal. The Chiron was more refined and quiet than its predecessor, the Bugatti Veyron, and was also surprisingly docile at low speeds.

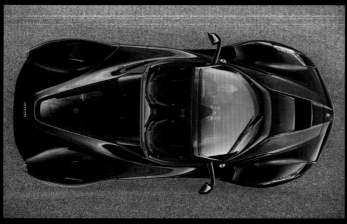

2017
FERRARI
LAFERRARI

Ferrari would probably be the last make expected to sell a hybrid, but the LaFerrari was no ordinary hybrid—it combined a 788-horsepower V-12 with a 161-hp electric motor for a total 949 hp. Introduced for 2013, the LaFerrari hybrid was even faster than Ferrari's celebrated 2003-04 Enzo model—it could rocket from 0-60 mph in less than three seconds and hit a top speed of 217 mph. Plus, the weight of the low-mounted battery packs lowered the car's center of gravity and improved handling. The LaFerrari's price tag was a cool $1.4 million, but Ferrari had no trouble selling 500 coupes, as well as 210 Aperta convertible versions. The final LaFerrari Aperta was sold at an auction in 2017 for $9.96 million, with proceeds supporting the Save the Children charity.

2017 FORD GT

Le Mans victory, Ford designed an all-new GT racecar for the 2016 24 Hours of Le Mans. The new GTs did their legendary forebears proud, finishing first, third, fourth, and ninth in the GTE Pro Class. The production GT was closely related to the racing version, and lacked the luxury features often found on other high-end supercars. The GT's cockpit was a tight fit for two passengers, and cargo room was almost nonexistent. The payoff was reduced weight, with racecar-like performance and handling. The EcoBoost 3.5-liter V6 shared its basic engine block with the Ford F-150, but developed 647 horsepower and was capable of traveling from 0-60 mph in 2.9 seconds and reaching a top speed of 216 mph, according to *Car and Driver*. The price was around $450,000, and Ford planned to build 1000 examples over the 2017–2020 model years.

2018
MCLAREN
720S

Although McLaren Automotive had its roots in racing, the McLaren 720S wasn't an uncomfortable, uncompromising performance car. In fact, the 720S was one of the most civilized supercars, boasting a quiet, smooth ride and docile manners in around-town driving. However, that doesn't mean that this English-built, mid-engine supercar lacked speed; its twin-turbo 4.0-liter V-8 developed 710 horsepower and was capable of 212 mph. Zero-60 mph took 2.8 seconds, and 0-100 mph came in only 5.5 seconds. Extensive use of carbon fiber helped bring the curb weight down to a reasonable 2828 pounds, and a computer-controlled active suspension provided both a comfortable ride and excellent handling. The 720S's base price was around $285,000.